Dan Reiland is known for coaching church l... tured the process he uses to develop local church leaders in this book. I highly recommend *Amplified Leadership*. I'm confident it will help you and your church go to the next level!

—CRAIG GROESCHEL
PASTOR OF LIFECHURCH.TV AND
AUTHOR OF *WEIRD: BECAUSE NORMAL ISN'T WORKING*
EDMOND, OK

Reaching more people for Jesus depends on your ability to develop new leaders. *Amplified Leadership* will help you do that. Dan Reiland loves the local church and is a true field-level practitioner. He leads leaders. Dan's book will give you a five-part and relationally based process to raise up new leaders. I highly recommend his book to you.

—PERRY NOBLE
SENIOR PASTOR OF NEWSPRING CHURCH
ANDERSON, SC

Dan Reiland is one of the best I have ever seen in helping church leaders reach their highest potential. Prediction: this work will become a textbook on practical leadership for tons of leaders.

—SHAWN LOVEJOY
COFOUNDER OF CHURCHPLANTERS.COM
LEAD PASTOR OF MOUNTAIN LAKE CHURCH
CUMMING, GA

As a leader who volunteers in my church and serves as a board member, I am very aware of the great need to find and develop leaders in a church. Dan's book will help you do just that!

—BOB TAYLOR
PRESIDENT AND COFOUNDER OF TAYLOR GUITARS

Dan Reiland is a leader of leaders. He has personally demonstrated how to cultivate leaders who encourage, challenge, and strengthen one another. *Amplified Leadership* is a practical, specific, and powerful guide for those who aren't content to settle for short-term impact and who desire to create a clear path for next-generation leaders.

—REGGIE JOINER
CEO OF THE reThink GROUP AND
FOUNDER OF THE ORANGE CONFERENCES

No one argues against the need for new and competent leaders. But if that's the case, why do churches struggle in this area? My friend Dan Reiland has put his finger on the issue in *Amplified Leadership*. Dan helps us understand the cyclical nature of processing relationships in a systematic and sequential manner to produce a harvest of leaders in any church. No manipulation, programs, or laborious efforts—just a way of life. Reading this book connects the dots and highlights the various landmarks in the journey toward being an effective leader by pointing the reader in the right direction and giving them fuel (motivation) to achieve the desired outcome.

—SAMUEL R. CHAND
AUTHOR OF CRACKING YOUR CHURCH'S CULTURE CODE

The most important metric of a healthy church is the number of leaders being developed. Do this well and everything else will take care of itself. *Amplified Leadership* is more than a book; it is a comprehensive and practical leadership-development toolkit. Applying these proven principles may be the most important step you take to open the leadership pipeline in your ministry.

—STEVE MOORE
PRESIDENT AND CEO OF THE MISSION EXCHANGE
AUTHOR OF WHO IS MY NEIGHBOR?: BEING A GOOD SAMARITAN
IN A CONNECTED WORLD

I've known Dan Reiland for a long time because I pastor the church where Dan was executive pastor for many years. His thumbprint is still on Skyline Church. In all candor, he is one of the most skilled church leaders I have ever seen. Dan has developed hundreds of effective church leaders, and now you can use the process that has worked so well at a grassroots level in the local church.

He's a trusted spiritual leader who loves the church and developing leaders. *Amplified Leadership* is a gift to you and your church.

—DR. JIM GARLOW
SENIOR PASTOR OF SKYLINE WESLEYAN CHURCH
SAN DIEGO, CA

Dan Reiland knows leadership, and this remarkable book proves it. If you're looking for practical and proven ways to improve your effectiveness as a leader, buy this book. Read it. And put it to work. You'll see measurable payoffs, and so will the people around you— sooner than you think. I can't recommend *Amplified Leadership* more strongly!

—LES PARROTT, PhD
FOUNDER OF REALRELATIONSHIPS.COM
AUTHOR OF *LOVE TALK*

When I think about developing leaders in a local church, I think Dan Reiland! He's done it. His track record for leadership development in growing churches is outstanding. Now you can take advantage of Dan's leadership expertise through his book *Amplified Leadership*. It teaches that developing leaders is a process that starts with establishing a good relationship and moves to empowerment! Take it from me, this book is a must if you want to develop leaders!

—DR. STAN TOLER
BEST-SELLING AUTHOR AND GENERAL SUPERINTENDENT OF THE
CHURCH OF THE NAZARENE

Amplified Leadership is long overdue. It is a manual any pastor can use to develop a culture of leaders in the church. As a guy who has committed his career to nurturing emerging leaders, I love how Dan has simplified the actions to transferable concepts. Further, it's not just theory. I've watched Dan Reiland practice these truths intentionally for decades. Thanks for putting your lifestyle into words, Dan.

—DR. TIM ELMORE
PRESIDENT OF GROWINGLEADERS.COM

This is the book for the church in this century! If you follow the pattern outlined in this book, you will see Spirit-led leaders developed exponentially in your church. Community to global transformation will result.

—JO ANNE LYON
GENERAL SUPERINTENDENT OF THE WESLEYAN CHURCH
FOUNDER/CHAIR OF WORLD HOPE INTERNATIONAL

Leadership is about more than inspiration. It takes the perspiration of investing your life into someone else. My longtime friend Dan Reiland has done this over and over, and *Amplified Leadership* shows us the way.

—DAVE TRAVIS
MANAGING DIRECTOR OF LEADERSHIP NETWORK

If you're a football player, the ultimate coach is Sir Alex Ferguson CBE. If you are a rugby player, that person is Sir Clive Woodward OBE. If you are a pastor, then he is Dan Reiland. Do everything in your power to have lunch with this man (like I did) because his wisdom will leave an impression on you for the rest of your leadership days. You will leave empowered to ignite someone's world. Failing that, buy this book. You'll get more than he could tell you in a dozen lunches!

—SIMON JARVIS
PASTOR OF ONE CHURCH GLOUCESTER
GLOUCESTER, ENGLAND

For more than thirty years Dan Reiland has been leading large and influential congregations. Central to his increasing influence is Dan's emphasis on developing leaders and involves enfolding those leaders into effective teams. Dan has become the go-to "leadership coach" to thousands of pastors across the country. What I most appreciate about Dan is that he is a leadership practitioner, not just another leadership professor. Dan lives daily in the arena of leadership realities, not simply leadership theories. *Amplified Leadership* is Dan Reiland's definitive work on a subject he passionately loves and lives out daily—leadership!

—Dr. John Hull
President/CEO of EQUIP Leadership

Recommending a book by Dan Reiland is easy for me. Dan is thorough. He has the unique ability to see through the layers of ministry, providing a clear view of the critical issues involved. Dan's approach to leadership is holistic. As he expounds the principles of leadership, he does more than grow the organization. He grows the leader. And Dan has been there. Whatever he writes, it is from the perspective of the daily grind. He has lived it, both the good and the bad. His thoughts are not theoretical; they have been proven true over time.

—Gerald Brooks
Senior Pastor of Grace Outreach Center
Plano, TX

Dan Reiland has given us a powerful tool for the ongoing leadership development of church teams. He has always been an outstanding strategic thinker and leader. *Amplified Leadership* communicates the practical principles for developing new leaders in your organization and a process for the continued growth of those leaders.

—Dr. Tom Mullins
Founding and Senior Pastor of Christ Fellowship
Palm Beach Gardens, FL

AMPLIFIED
LEADERSHIP

AMPLIFIED
LEADERSHIP

DAN REILAND

CHARISMA
HOUSE

Most CHARISMA HOUSE BOOK GROUP products are available at special quantity discounts for bulk purchase for sales promotions, premiums, fundraising, and educational needs. For details, write Charisma House Book Group, 600 Rinehart Road, Lake Mary, Florida 32746, or telephone (407) 333-0600.

AMPLIFIED LEADERSHIP by Dan Reiland
Published by Charisma House
Charisma Media/Charisma House Book Group
600 Rinehart Road
Lake Mary, Florida 32746
www.charismahouse.com

Unless otherwise noted, all Scripture quotations are from the Holy Bible, New International Version. Copyright © 1973, 1978, 1984, International Bible Society. Used by permission.

Scripture quotations marked NKJV are from the New King James Version of the Bible. Copyright © 1979, 1980, 1982 by Thomas Nelson, Inc. Used by permission. All rights reserved.

Cover design by Justin Evans
Design Director: Bill Johnson

Visit the author's website at http://danreiland.com.

12Stone® Church is a registered trademark.

Library of Congress Cataloging-in-Publication Data:
Reiland, Dan.
  Amplified leadership / Dan Reiland. -- 1st ed.
    p. cm.
  ISBN 978-1-61638-472-2 (trade paper) -- ISBN 978-1-61638-635-1 (e-book) 1.
Christian leadership. I. Title.
  BV652.1.R455 2011
  253--dc23
                                                2011039133

12 13 14 15 16 — 9 8 7 6 5 4 3 2
Printed in the United States of America

To the leaders of 12Stone Church,

who are:

courageous in spirit,

generous by nature,

and passionate about Jesus.

CONTENTS

Acknowledgments

I T HAS BEEN said that nothing worthwhile is accomplished alone. I think that's true. Many people helped make this book possible or offered advice that made it better, and for each one I am sincerely grateful.

Thank you, Kevin Myers, for your visionary leadership and encouragement to get this book written. *Amplified Leadership* is better because of our ministry partnership.

Great thanks to Charlie Wetzel. You are a brilliant writer and a patient friend. Thank you for listening to me talk about this book for so many years and for offering so many great suggestions. This book wouldn't have been the same without your rich wisdom.

I also want to thank Richie Hughes, my literary agent. Who would have guessed a lunch at P. F. Chang's would lead to a friendship and some cool new endeavors? Thanks for catching the vision for this book and walking with me until it became a reality.

Much gratitude to Lesley Lewis, my always cheerful assistant who reviewed this manuscript over and over again and somehow *remained* cheerful. Thank you for keeping track of all the details. Because of you, I'm still sane!

A big shout-out goes to Lisa Huff, Miles Welch, and Robin Ritchie. Your sharp eyes and keen minds helped fine-tune the manuscript and made it presentable to the publisher.

Thanks to the entire team at Charisma House. Your expertise and partnership took the book to another level. And a special thanks to Adrienne Gaines, my editor. You truly made this a better book.

I must also thank my longtime friend and leadership mentor John Maxwell, who wrote such a gracious foreword. Without you, I'd have nothing to say on leadership.

To my daughter, Mackenzie, and my son, John-Peter—thank you for loving me despite the gazillion times I brought up this book at the dinner table. I know you are truly happy it's done.

And finally, to Patti, my beautiful bride. Thank you for thirty wonderful years and for still believing in me.

Foreword

FIRST MET DAN and Patti Reiland when they were just "kids" out of seminary. We shared an instant rapport that resulted in Dan joining me on staff at Skyline Wesleyan Church in San Diego, California. Neither of us knew that would launch a twenty-year working relationship and a lifetime friendship.

When I met Dan I knew he was smart, had a deep love for people, and possessed an innate understanding of how a local church worked. But he was very green as a leader and had much to learn. I knew he needed intentional development as a leader. He started working with me as an intern in 1982. He finished as my executive pastor, leading all the staff and ministries of the church. He understands leadership development because he was developed.

You need to know a little about me so you can know why I

care so much about Dan and this book. I was a pastor for twenty-five years. I served in three churches, two in Ohio and one in California. As a young pastor I remember my first church in a little town called Hillham, Indiana. I thought I had all the answers to leadership, and I quickly discovered I had much to learn. I was a rookie leader then. I immediately developed a passionate hunger for someone to coach me as a leader.

I remember getting my hands on the book *Spiritual Leadership* by J. Oswald Sanders. The principles jumped off the pages. It changed my life. I discovered that others knew much more about leadership than I did. I began to seek out leaders who would teach me what they knew. To this day I am grateful for those who poured leadership into me and helped make the churches I led successful. That's partly why, since the end of that twenty-five-year era in my life, I've dedicated myself to teaching others about leadership.

I've met literally thousands of pastors in my life. The vast majority have been good and godly men and women who are devoutly spiritual people. They pray, love people, and work very hard, but their churches lack results. There is a reason most churches in the country have fewer than one hundred people. There is a reason churches grow to five hundred or five thousand and then stop growing. It's always about leadership. Everything rises and falls on leadership. Next to the kindness and favor of God, leadership is the difference maker.

You may be a good leader, but even that is not enough. You must find and develop other leaders because you can't do it all yourself. That's where *Amplified Leadership* comes in. It's a relationally based process that starts with establishing a relationship and ends with an empowered leader.

Dan is one of the best at developing leaders that I know. I've watched him do it for decades. He is gifted in his ability to break down an intuitive process into bite-size, transferable pieces so that others can duplicate it. This book is filled with veteran-level insights from a guy who has used it to train hundreds of leaders.

Read this book, follow the process, and develop your leaders. You will not be disappointed in the results. My prayer is that you will keep your heart hot for God, love people, continue to grow as a leader—and become a champion of developing new leaders!

—JOHN C. MAXWELL

John C. Maxwell is a best-selling author and founder of The John Maxwell Company and EQUIP, organizations that have trained more than five million leaders worldwide.

Introduction

DON'T ENTER THE RING UNPREPARED

CINDERELLA MAN IS one of my favorite movies. In it Russell Crowe plays James J. Braddock, a prizefighter down on his luck during the Great Depression. Braddock was determined to provide for his family, so he returned to the ring at a time when most people thought his career was over. To everyone's surprise, Braddock scored win after win. Then he did the unthinkable.

On June 13, 1935, in Long Island City, New York, Braddock faced off against Max Baer, the heavyweight champion of the world. Baer was more than a fierce opponent; he was a dangerous fighter who had reportedly killed two men in the ring. But Braddock was fighting for more than a title. He was fighting for food to feed his kids, for dignity, and for the country he believed in. He was fighting for all the people who needed hope. For Braddock, the stakes were much higher than surviving fifteen rounds at Madison Square Garden.

I can relate a little to the Cinderella Man. I've been in the "ring" for nearly thirty years, giving it my best shot in ministry. Like Braddock's match, the fight we're in is much bigger than it appears. It's not just about one local church or ministry organization—yours or mine. It's about the global church and the hope it can give to a broken world. It's a fight for the church to experience its finest hour.

I know a church or ministry's success ultimately rests upon the kindness and favor of God, but I've learned something else in my years as a church leader and pastors' coach. I've found that the long-term potential of a church or ministry largely depends on a minister's ability to develop new and competent leaders. That is what compelled me to write this book.

This book isn't for the casual leader. It is for the strong and courageous. It is for those who have chosen not to sit in a spectator's chair, who are committed to stay in the ring fighting for a cause they believe in—the cause of Christ. Our opponent is daunting, but together we can win the fight.

This book isn't a fable. It's not an allegory. And there is no clever ending. It's based on the real stories of dozens of churches and hundreds of ministry leaders who are willing to go one more round because the cause is worth it.

I love the body of Christ. I love the Bridegroom, who is our true Champion. I love all of you leaders who are in the ring, male and female, giving it everything you've got. I'm writing this book in hopes of helping you hit a little harder and last a lot longer. And I especially want to encourage young leaders who have only recently stepped into the ring. All great fighters need a trainer for coaching and instruction. And they need someone who believes in them, someone who is in their corner. I hope this book is all that for you.

Yes, you're the leader, but you can't do it all on your own. You must grow in your leadership role and develop other leaders around you. A good coach helps fighters strengthen their muscles, learn proper timing, and sharpen their instincts. I want to do something similar for you by offering five key leadership practices and ten corresponding skill sets that will help you go the distance.

Practical skills are only one of four dimensions of leadership. There is also a spiritual dimension, a psychological dimension, and an organizational dimension. And all four components build on a foundation of relationship. I will touch upon all the dimensions of leadership in this book, and those leading any kind of ministry organization will be able to glean from this process. But because *Amplified Leadership* was born out of my years leading in local churches and coaching pastors, it focuses especially on the leadership skills needed for effective ministry in the local church.

One of the unique contributions of this book is that it puts the five leadership practices into a progressive sequence, and it connects the desired results with the necessary skill sets. The chart below outlines the outcomes and skills we will cover in this book.

LEADERSHIP OUTCOME DESIRED	LEADERSHIP SKILL SETS REQUIRED
Establish a Relationship	Connect and Appreciate
Engage a Follower	Encourage and Inspire
Embrace a Team Member	Invite and Equip
Coach an Apprentice	Select and Include
Mentor a New Leader	Develop and Empower

Amplified Leadership is a relationally based process designed to intentionally cultivate new leaders. It is not merely a list of activities leaders engage in. It is a specific sequence of practical steps that lead to a strategic outcome—producing new leaders.

This process acknowledges that the vast majority of ministry leaders, both staff and volunteer, will demonstrate their leadership through the relationships they create and sustain, not necessarily by casting vision from a platform. Typically the senior leader is tasked with communicating the vision, especially within the context of a local church. But all leaders must establish relationships and mentor others if the church is to develop the large number of leaders needed to minister to those who are lost and hurting.

This book begins with the end in mind. It first teaches leaders how to connect relationally with a significant number of people, then to engage followers from those relationships. From the followers, the leaders learn to embrace team members, and from the team they select apprentice leaders to coach. Then, finally, the leader is able to mentor new leaders. When a new leader is developed, he or she must repeat the process by establishing new relationships. I call this process *Amplified Leadership* because its purpose is to continually develop new leaders who will help increase and expand your ministry, resulting in more changed lives in Jesus's name.

Character Matters

If you saw *Cinderella Man*, you know that Braddock was a man of integrity, and that made a big difference in the decisions he made. Before I launch into Part One, I want to talk about the kind of leader who steps into the ring and fights the good fight. That individual is a person of character. No matter how well you master the skill sets I discuss in this book, they will be worth little if you lack character. Leaders reproduce who they are, not what they do.

A spiritual leader must live a life worth being replicated. The process of developing new leaders is not like manufacturing a car. Human beings behave according to an internal set of ethics and morals that are more caught than taught. If you are a leader, people watch you. This is a good thing. So often this reality is described negatively as "fishbowl living." This is only negative if we have to pretend and behave differently than we would if no one was looking. People will trust us more if we live godly lives and let people "catch" us doing the right things.

Integrity always prevails over personality. A person may have amazing charisma, but in the end character will determine his or her success as a leader. Modeling godly character does not have to be difficult. Just keep these principles in mind:

Live by the same standard you expect of others.

Few things reveal a breakdown in character more than when a leader doesn't live by the standard he preaches about—unless he lives according to a *higher* standard. (See 1 Timothy 3:1–10). When a leader believes he has risen above the rules of right living and begins to make exceptions to accommodate a sinful lifestyle, his leadership will eventually reveal the cracks in his character.

Character is revealed not only in the big issues of life such as marriage, finances, and career, but also in the small things. In *Cinderella Man*, a reporter from the *Boston Globe* interviewed James Braddock and asked him why he returned the federal relief money he had received before he began earning an income from boxing. Braddock said: "I believe we live in a great country, a country that's great enough to help a man financially when he is in trouble, but lately I've had some good fortune, and I'm back in the black, and I just thought that I should return it."[1] No one would have known if he had kept his relief money. And if anyone did know, he probably would have told Braddock to keep it to buy some extra milk for his kids. But character always helps you do the right thing.

Leaders with character do not set themselves above the people. They roll up their sleeves, get involved, and show the way. Those of us who are leaders are the models, the ones people look to as examples. So we must live in a way that is worthy of the high calling of leadership. This is not about perfection; it's about a having a heart that is sold out to a godly way of life.

Depend on God and allow the Holy Spirit's power into the process.

Life is not always easy, and our character is often challenged. Do you remember the story of Job in the Old Testament? He had a great family, wealth, and generally a good life. So Satan challenged God and said in essence, "Yes, Job is righteous because life is easy for him. Let me make his life difficult, and see what happens." God allowed Satan to have access to Job, but with the condition that Satan could not hurt Job physically.

So the attack began. Job's livestock was stolen, his servants were slaughtered, and while his children were having a party, the wind blew his house down, killing all of his sons and daughters. It can't get much worse than that. Yet Job did not blame God. In fact, Job chose to worship Him (Job 1:20–22). Until the day Job died, he never allowed his character to crumble despite having to endure personal attacks (Job 27:5–6).

No matter how great our leadership ability may be, life will present challenges that remind us of our dependence upon God.

Although each of us has been given gifts and talents, without the power of God we can do little that lasts. *Only* the power of God enables us to keep our character intact. We must lean into God's grace, love, and power. And we must pray. Our best connection to God's power is on our knees in sweet conversation with Him. He is our source, our righteousness, our character—our all in all. Without Him, we can hang up our gloves because the fight is over.

A Note About Terminology

I must digress for a moment and make a comment about the terminology I will use in *Amplified Leadership*. I realize "volunteer" is not an ideal term for those who serve in ministry. Spiritually, followers of Jesus are not volunteers; they are servants who are called, gifted, and empowered by God.

However, both organizationally and practically, the people who serve in a local church or ministry setting are volunteers. When someone serves a body of believers, it is by his or her own choice. The person is not drafted; he volunteers. So in a spiritual sense, believers are not volunteers, but in a practical and organizational way they are.

Even if you prefer a word other than volunteer, I hope you will allow me this latitude. I pray my use of the term will not prevent you from receiving the greatest value from this book. Now, let's begin.

PART
ONE

ESTABLISH A RELATIONSHIP

Relationship is the cornerstone of enduring leadership.

U NCOMMON FRIENDS IS a good book written by real estate developer James Newton. Drawing from his journals, memories, and extensive correspondence, Newton writes warmly and candidly about his lifelong friendships with inventor Thomas Edison, businessmen Henry Ford and Harvey Firestone, Nobel Prize–winning biologist Alexis Carrel, and aviator Charles Lindbergh. What struck me about Newton's book was not that he developed long and deep friendships with such extraordinary people. What I found powerful—and uncommon—was that all of those busy and accomplished men spent so much time investing in their relationships.

If you were to write a book about your friends, whose names would you include? Even if you never write that book, a story is still being written. Your life is being written about in the hearts of those you love and care for most. Relationships are important to us all, and our friendships in particular are a powerful force in our lives. Our friends influence the people we become, for better or worse. Let me tell you a story about my daughter that will bring this truth to life.

It was as if the earth stood still and all the stars were in perfect alignment. There she was, my sixteen-year-old daughter, Mackenzie, standing at the bottom of the stairs wearing *a dress*. This was easily the eighth wonder of the world. Mackenzie is as cute as she can be and has always been a classic tomboy. She hates pink and refuses to have her nails done. Mackenzie is strictly a jeans and T-shirt kid.

No amount of pressure or money from mom or dad could get her in a formal dress—ever. Then came time for the homecoming dance. She had no intention of going. The United States Marines couldn't make her go. That was before several of her high school friends started working on her. They spent weeks chipping away at her resolve, and eventually they took her shopping. I was shocked when Mackenzie bought a beautiful formal dress. She came home, put it on, and looked stunning. Mackenzie is still our tomboy, but she has worn a dress a few times since then and looked gorgeous!

No matter how much my wife and I love Mackenzie and our son, John-Peter, or how much they love us, our children will forever be shaped by their friendships. In fact, one day they will give themselves in marriage to someone who started out as a friend. The power of friendship cannot be overestimated.

As leaders, we have to understand the incredible force of relational influence, or we will eventually be blindsided in our leadership. If we can't make and keep meaningful relationships, our effectiveness as leaders will be in jeopardy. This is particularly true in the local church environment, where successful leadership and ministry are literally built on relationships. This doesn't mean everyone should be your best friend or even a close friend. But genuine leadership requires relationship.

At the time of this writing, John Maxwell and I have been friends for nearly thirty years. I wouldn't trade my relationship with John for anything. He's like my older brother. He is also my mentor, confidant, adviser, and former pastor. When it comes to leadership, John has taught me much about the value of relationships. He has taught me lessons such as, "People don't care how much you know until they know how much you care," "Walk slowly through the crowds so you can pay attention to people," and "Always add value to everyone you meet." I have watched him live this. He leads in a way that consistently shows he cares about people. And he adds value to people's lives.

John has been a blessing and inspiration to me. However, our friendship hasn't been automatic. It has taken desire, effort, and intentionality on both our parts. From traveling the world together to advance the work of the church to attending a Paul McCartney concert with our wives, John and I have spent time cultivating a relationship that is rich and full. In the same way, you will get out of your relationships what you put into them.

THE BLESSING OF FRIENDSHIP

Friends are a blessing. You never know what will come from each relationship you begin. One of the many blessings of my relationship with John was the privilege of helping him write a little book titled *The Treasure of a Friend*. Consider this definition of friendship John and I shared in that book:

> Friendship is based on what it gives, not what it gets. Friendship stays alive by serving the other, not seeking to be served. Friendship is motivated by love, not debt. Friendship is willing to sacrifice without seeing or expecting a return. It doesn't make sense, but the more it gives up the stronger it gets.[1]

This is the core from which ministry leaders should approach establishing new relationships. Our priority should be what we give, not what we get. I know that as ministry leaders, we are about the mission of advancing the kingdom of God. We want to see the church flourish. We are willing to trade our lives for the Great Commission, which commands us to "go and make disciples of all nations" (Matt. 28:19). We are fired up about accomplishing God's purpose, no matter what it takes. But people don't exist to help us accomplish the mission; they *are* the mission. They are souls who must be treated with dignity and respect. Our leadership will rise to a new level when we genuinely see others as people we care about rather than as more work.

Leaders, motivated by love, are called to serve others. Good leaders desire to see the people they serve grow in their walk with Christ, and they want as many as possible to become leaders themselves. Yet loving leaders serve without strings attached. They know that not everyone they build relationships with will become leaders. This was the case with Jesus. When He walked the earth, Jesus served His friends without expecting anything in return (though on a divine level He desired their obedience and devotion). Yet when He chose twelve disciples from among His friends, He expected much of them because they were called to become leaders and serve as He did.

Although I know some pretty discerning leaders, most of us won't know who has leadership potential until we've spent time getting to know them and observing them in action. This is why relationship is so critical to the leadership development process. It is more than a first step; it is the foundation. If you're serious about increasing and expanding your leadership, you have to take the initiative to form new relationships. You can't sit back and wait for people to come to you. Regardless of your personality type, temperament, or energy level, it is up to you as a leader to make the first move.

Don't hold back. Pick up the phone and create a time and place for new relationships to blossom. And by all means, don't judge a book by its cover. It's easy to size people up before we get to know them. Resist that temptation and take a risk. Get to know people you might not normally engage with. More than likely, you'll be surprised by what you find.

I know that dozens, if not hundreds, of people cross your path every week, and you're probably wondering how you can know which ones to engage with. There's a very simple key. When we get up every morning, we must ask the Holy Spirit to prompt relational connections that bring God glory, advance the kingdom, and provide a platform for encouragement. We must trust the Holy Spirit to make divine appointments for us and select the people we build relationships with. This practice in tandem with having a strategic plan to invest time with the right people will deliver strong results.

Just as trust is key in our relationship with God, it is also central to leadership and nurturing significant relationships. Take a moment to reflect on another quote from *The Treasure of a Friend*:

> People's confidence in you springs from two things. The first
> is the trustworthiness of your character. The second is how
> responsible you are. The friends who trust you do so because
> they can count on you.[2]

Is this true of you? Can people count on you? Do you do what
you say you will do? Do you genuinely care about not only your
friends but also people in general? Can people trust that you will
put their interests above your own? Can they trust you to do the
right thing and get the job done? Every leader must ask himself
these questions and answer honestly. If you can answer yes to these
questions, you have a large part of the foundation of leadership
intact, and you likely are a good and trusted friend to many.

A COMPOUNDING INVESTMENT

So how does a leader manage what seems to be an unending and
unrealistic number of relationships? We have a finite amount
of time, yet we receive endless opportunities to engage with new
people. How does a leader keep up? The answer lies in the level of
investment you make into each relationship and how mature they
become. Relationships in their early stages require more time, but
as they mature, more meaningful connection can be made in less
time. Let me briefly explain what I mean.

Relationships are not linear; they are cumulative and exponential in nature. Like good investments, good relationships com-
pound in their earnings. They still require time, but the time
invested actually multiplies the value of the relationship. When we
have taken the time to get to know someone and understand who
they are and how they communicate, we will be able to respond to

their needs more quickly than with someone we just met. These more mature relationships free us up to establish new ones.

To be sure, developing relationships can be exhausting, and this reveals the inevitable tension in the relational art of leadership. People want more time than you have to give. This problem demands an answer. And the solution lies in establishing and nurturing relationships that are deep but not so involved that you create unrealistic expectations. You can't spend all of your time mentoring new leaders, but it is unwise to hold most, if not all, people emotionally at arm's length. This approach isn't relational. It's mechanical, and it will eventually hurt your ability to lead because the people following you won't be able to find your heart. A wise strategy is to invest more time in a smaller number of people and develop them into leaders who will turn around and invest time empowering others to lead. This is what it means to amplify your leadership.

Establishing new relationships is a nonnegotiable art all leaders must master. It is the first step in developing new leaders, and it requires two important skills: the ability to connect and the ability to appreciate people for who they are. When you develop these skills, you will not only experience the blessing of seeing the mission accomplished, but you will also discover the joy of walking together with friends on life's journey.

Chapter One

CONNECT AT THE HEART

Leadership begins at the place we connect—the heart.

S A LEADER, I want to find a person's heart as quickly as I can. The most certain way to do this is to give my heart first, but it's not always that easy. I'm sure there have been times when you just couldn't connect with someone. No matter how hard you tried, you couldn't find the real person inside. In these situations, one of two things was probably in play. Either the person was intentionally keeping you out, or you needed to increase your ability to create a connection. Sometimes it's a little of both. Whatever the case, it's up to you as the leader to take the initiative.

Chemistry plays an active part in helping people connect.

Natural chemistry is a highly coveted kind of "interpersonal magic." We all know it when we experience it, and it's easy to spot in local church environments. Every small group is a study in relational chemistry. The groups that experience natural chemistry can't seem to get enough of one another. After the small group meeting is over, they stay late just to hang out together. They don't leave until the third pot of coffee is completely empty and the last piece of cake is gone. The members stay in touch during the week and plan activities outside of the regular small group night.

> **Connection is the beginning of all true influence.**

Small groups without natural chemistry can be boring and lack energy. The only reason the members ask for coffee is to help them stay awake. The group members are late or don't show up at all, and eventually they stop attending. I have interviewed dozens upon dozens of people who left a small group because they just didn't connect with the leader or the members.

With that said, natural chemistry isn't everything. In fact, positive relational chemistry is often *cultivated* by a skilled leader who knows how important it is to increase connection. For example, as executive pastor at 12Stone Church I am responsible for the staff. I am well aware that each time I hire a key pastor or ministry director, I risk seeing a breakdown in team connection due to a lack of chemistry. If the new team member is a good leader and if I lead well, together we can cultivate chemistry even if it was absent initially. This takes effort and intentionality, but it is very doable. It's often no more complicated than creating time and space for people to genuinely get to know and appreciate one another.

Connection is the beginning of all true influence. It's like the "Go" square in the game Monopoly. If you don't connect, you do not pass go and do not take any people with you. Meaningful friendships require deep connections. There's just no way around it. So how do you strengthen your ability to connect? It's not as difficult as you may think. In this chapter we will discuss several traits that will either help or hinder your ability to create warm and genuine connections and build lasting relationships.

AUTHENTICITY VS. SELF-PROTECTION

Connection is largely about being real, but it doesn't end there. Someone who is not a leader can be real and connect with people, but he will not necessarily add value to a person's life. A leader connects, cares, and adds value. He never leaves the table without seeking to have made a positive contribution. This all begins with personal authenticity, and the greatest blockage to this kind of transparency is self-protection.

Self-protection is rooted in fear and results in hiding.

Genesis 3 tells a story of self-protection. Adam and Eve were created to exist in perfect relationship with God. But the first couple gave in to temptation, and their sin broke the communion they had with God. Instead of trying to reconnect with the Father, Adam and Eve tried to hide from Him.

> When the woman saw that the fruit of the tree was good for food and pleasing to the eye, and also desirable for gaining wisdom, she took some and ate it. She also gave some to her husband, who was with her, and he ate it. Then the eyes of both of them were opened, and they realized they were naked; so they sewed fig leaves together and made coverings for themselves. Then the man and his wife heard the sound

of the LORD God as he was walking in the garden in the cool
of the day, and they hid from the LORD God among the trees
of the garden. But the LORD God called to the man, "Where
are you?" He answered, "I heard you in the garden, and I was
afraid because I was naked; so I hid."

—GENESIS 3:6–10

Adam and Eve chose to hide, as if God wouldn't be able to
see them. Leaders often do the same thing for various reasons.
Sometimes we're afraid the people we lead will catch us in our sin. I
remember when my son, John-Peter, was about three years old, and
his mother and I told him not to get a cookie. Instead of being obedient, he chose to get one anyway. When I walked into the kitchen,
there he stood with an Oreo in one hand and the lid to the cookie
jar in the other. When I asked him if he took a cookie, he moved
the hand with the cookie behind his back and said, "No."

I couldn't help but laugh at my three-year-old son, but it's not
so funny when a leader gets caught with his or her hand in the
cookie jar. It's even worse when a leader denies his or her wrong-
doing when confronted. Leaders who fall into sin do damage to
themselves and the ministries they serve. Truly effective leaders
must live the same truth they preach.

That brings me to another reason leaders attempt to hide from
the people they serve. Oftentimes we don't want to be caught being
ourselves. I knew a young and talented pastor who was operating
as if he was an extrovert because he thought all great leaders were
extroverts. As any true introvert would experience in this scenario,
this pastor began to exhaust himself. Two members of the church
board lovingly confronted him, yet he insisted he was an extrovert.

The pastor never allowed himself to get the quiet time he so
desperately needed to refuel and refresh. As a result, he became

chronically cranky and eventually very angry. After months of this, and repeated heart-to-heart conversations, the church asked him to resign. If the pastor had been willing to be himself, he likely would have enjoyed a long and productive ministry.

Self-protection wastes emotional energy.

Just as a computer has a certain amount of memory, your emotional constitution has only so much energy. It is futile to pretend to be anyone other than the person God created you to be. When I was a young leader, I noticed that many leaders had a combination of choleric and sanguine temperaments. So I thought I should have that temperament also, and I attempted to mimic it. I didn't realize that I noticed these outgoing individuals partially because of their personality and not necessarily their leadership. My temperament is a combination of choleric and melancholy. But until I gave myself permission to be myself—and discovered that I enjoyed being myself—I wasn't able to really make lasting connections.

Self-protection is an attempt to control circumstances.

Adam and Eve thought putting on clothes would change their situation, but that didn't work. If anything, their attempt to "fix" the awkward moment their sin created caused more separation between themselves and God. Fear is conquered by authenticity, not self-protection. You become truly authentic when you discover that people can and will accept you for who you are. When this happens, real connection is all but guaranteed.

Authenticity requires you to be yourself.

Not everyone will like you. This is just a part of life. But those who do will like you best when you are being authentically yourself. You can't make everyone happy; in fact, that's not your job. A leader is not called to make people happy but to make people better.

And consider this: when you lie awake at night worried about what someone might be thinking about you, that person is most likely sleeping peacefully. Stop worrying about what other people will think of you. Let it go, and give yourself permission to be yourself. You are at your best when you are being yourself.

Authenticity requires that you trust God.

I've never doubted that God knew what He was doing when He made me, but on more than one occasion I have felt like Moses. I have thought God called me to do something I was not capable of accomplishing. I didn't find a total release from that anxiety until I realized an important truth. I was right! I am not capable of fulfilling the calling on my life without God.

Leaders push the edge to take new territory, and we all need God's help to do this. He has given us gifts, and He knows what He's doing. The tough part is to properly assess ourselves. I'm not talking about analyzing our performance. I'm talking about examining whether we are being the person God called us to be. The best way to know this is to take the inner-peace test. This is simple to do. Just ask yourself if you have a sense of inner peace. Having inner peace does not mean you lack external stress. It means you have peace in your soul. You know when you have it and when you don't. You will never have peace if you pretend to be someone you're not. You must be yourself.

Authenticity requires community.

It is often said that true community requires authenticity. But it's also true that you can't express authenticity outside of community. Authenticity requires healthy relationships. As a leader, you need a small group of friends, perhaps three to five, who give you absolute permission to be yourself at all times. If you get "off track" in some way, someone in the group will be there to let you know. This increases your ability to be self-aware and improves your comfort level with your true self. This honest and healthy feedback from your circle of friends will give you confidence to express yourself without fear when you are in less familiar territory—a place leaders know all too well.

> **Good leadership begins with authenticity.**

I invite you to take a minute to assess yourself. Are you being real as a leader? I have spent a lot of time talking about authenticity because if you don't get this, the rest of this chapter will be futile. You don't have to win the battle against self-protection overnight, but attempt to become more authentic every day. If you believe you already have this idea mastered, then push yourself a little further. Ask yourself how you can leverage your unique qualities as a leader to add value to people's lives and accomplish the vision God has given you.

INTIMACY VS. DISTANCE

Intimacy is a close cousin to authenticity. At its core, intimacy is about trust. The people I experience the most intimate relationships with are those I trust the most. The same is true for you as a leader. Trust determines whether people feel close to you and will be willing to follow you. Below is a relational sequence I urge you to learn:

Heart → Connect → Trust → Follow

Good leadership begins with authenticity. When you are yourself, people can connect with your heart. When they connect with

15

you, they are able to trust you. And when they trust you, they will follow you. Let me say this in reverse so you get the full impact. People will not follow leaders they do not trust. People don't trust leaders they can't connect with, and people can't connect with leaders if they can't find their heart.

A few years ago I had lunch with a pastor who has always had a big heart. During our lunch, he told me about a situation with a local bank president who oversaw a large loan for his church. He and the bank president had been friends for years, and the pastor often willingly signed contracts that in most ways were in the bank's favor. He never believed in a million years that this would become a problem. But when the church needed more money, without any explanation the banker seemed to turn on him and the church by applying undue pressure for repayment of the balance of the current loan. The pastor was deeply wounded by the unexpected turn of events and responded by telling me, "Never again will I trust people like that."

It's understandable that this pastor would be hurt by the banker's actions, but distancing himself from people is not the answer. Many pastors think they can protect themselves this way, but the wall that keeps people away also cuts leaders off from the love and support of the people they're called to serve. And it prevents leaders from sharing their love and care with the people around them.

When it comes to trust, leaders must go first. Trust sets the stage for meaningful relationship by opening the doors of people's hearts. When the people you lead see that you trust them, they are much more apt to trust you. If you are an experienced leader, you know that eventually you will be embarrassed, frustrated, or even betrayed by someone you lead. But you must resist the temptation to stop trusting people. Trust allows you to reveal your heart and gives others a chance to experience your true leadership.

Intimacy can be scary, and it requires risk, but the reward is well worth it. Charlie Wetzel is a trusted and close friend of mine. He is an elder at 12Stone Church, his wife, Stephanie, was my administrative assistant when I was on staff at a church in San Diego, and he is my prayer partner. We are also connected through John Maxwell because Charlie works with John on various projects. I tell Charlie just about everything. In fact, he knows so much about me, he could extort me for all the money I have and everything I might ever earn! Is my openness with Charlie a risk? Yes. But it's also one of the most rewarding relationships anyone could possibly enjoy. I can completely be myself with him without compromising my leadership role in his life. We both speak truthfully and enjoy a rich friendship. I always know Charlie has my back. This would not be possible if I opted to maintain a safe distance rather than risk intimacy.

SHOWING WARMTH AND CONCERN VS. BEING COLD AND ALOOF

Several years ago Donald Miller, author of *Blue Like Jazz* and other great books, spoke at 12Stone Church. It's always fun to have a "famous" person come to town, but you never know what they're really like until you get close up. My daughter, Mackenzie, was reading *Blue Like Jazz*, so I invited her to sit next to Don and me. When she sat down, I introduced Don to her and asked him if he would sign her book.

He could have easily and appropriately given Mackenzie a polite hello and asked her how she would like him to sign her book. Instead, he beamed that disarming smile of his and said, "Hey,

Mackenzie, good to meet you. Where do you go to school?" He spent the next several minutes asking Mackenzie about her life and interests, and then he signed her book. That's all it took. In three or four minutes he had two new friends, and we became his fans for life.

Part of the foundation of warmth and concern is genuinely caring about the people you serve. This is not something that can be learned from a book; I can only remind you of the vital importance of this basic truth. Caring about people causes you to go the second (and third) mile, not because you feel obligated but because you genuinely care. People know when you care, and they perceive that as warmth and concern.

Dr. Bill Martin is a brilliant physician who attends 12Stone. He founded the Hope Clinic, a nonprofit organization in Lawrenceville, Georgia, with a vision to help people who can't afford medical insurance. Doctors, especially Dr. Martin, are busy, and most of us have experienced at least one physician who had the bedside manner of King Kong and the personality of cold blue steel. Not so with Dr. Martin. He always makes you feel like you are the most important person in the world and that his purpose for living is to serve you. His personal warmth and genuine concern for people are magnanimous and reassuring.

Showing warmth and concern means paying attention to relational details. Some leaders are simply not detail-oriented, but when it comes to people, details can make you or break you. If you connect with someone on Sunday morning and say you'll call during the week, you'd better call. If you promise to send a book, do some research, reserve a room, or whatever—do it. The person you connected with doesn't view those offers as small and unimportant tasks. In fact, he will take it personally if you fail to follow through with the task, no matter how small it is, because it matters to him. To forget the task is to forget the person. Write it down if you need to, or ask someone to remind you to do it. It's better to not make the offer than to promise something and not follow through.

Leaders who are cool toward people most likely aren't communicating the disposition of their heart. Some leaders are aloof because of insecurity, fear, lack of concern, or emotional detachment. I strongly suggest these individuals seek wise counsel to address the root issue. More often, however, aloofness is a symptom of an overworked leader who needs to take some time for rest and exercise. I know many leaders who are exhausted because they aren't taking care of themselves. Because of their personal stress, they see people as an added drain on their lives. They fail to see the opportunity God has given them to serve. You have to be "filled up" yourself before you can give to others. Take time to refuel on a regular basis so you can give yourself away.

So how about you? As a leader, would people describe you as cool and aloof or warm and full of concern for those around you? Your answer to that question makes all the difference in how well you connect with the people you hope to lead. If you aren't naturally warm and caring, practice asking meaningful questions of the people you connect with and really listen to their answers. That is a good first step toward developing meaningful relationships and strong friendships.

IDENTIFICATION VS. INDEPENDENCE

People connect with (and ultimately follow) leaders they believe are like them in some way, even if the similarity is minimal. This is core to identification. People identify with something about you such as a belief, a passion, or even a favorite band. The first time

I spoke at 12Stone Church, I brought in an original, autographed copy of Crosby, Stills and Nash's 1969 self-titled album as a sermon illustration. That was many years ago, and I'd be willing to bet that no one who was there that Sunday would remember what I spoke about. Yet people often ask me if I still have that "cool album."

Identification vs. independence is easy to grasp until you start trying to figure out how much self-disclosure is appropriate. It's one thing to be real; it's quite another to be weird. Too much information too fast is not good. So where do we draw the line? What should a leader share and what should be withheld? When I reach this point during my coaching sessions, inexperienced leaders often tell me, "I thought you said to be real!" That's true, but I didn't say to tell people about your hemorrhoid surgery minutes after you meet them.

Self-disclosure is an art. Little kids and senior citizens entertain me because they typically have no limits on their self-disclosure. They say whatever they want, to whomever they want, whenever they want. Leaders don't have that privilege. It's almost impossible for me to say where you should draw the line because every situation is unique. What I can do is give you some guiding principles.

First, ask yourself why you are telling the story about yourself. Is it because no one will listen to you at home? Is it for self-catharsis, so you might feel better? Or are you telling the story because you are still discovering who you are and you want to convince others of your discovery? These questions aren't meant to intimidate you but to help you get honest about your reasons for wanting to tell the story. If you answered yes to any of the previous questions, you probably shouldn't tell the story. But there are four good reasons for you to share stories about yourself:

- **To instruct.** Telling personal stories can help people relate to the principle you are teaching.

- **To entertain.** All good communicators understand the value of humor, regardless of whether the communication is one-on-one or before a group. Moments of humor help people lower their defenses and increase their receptivity to the point being made.

- **To inspire.** A personal story is one of the best ways to inspire people. It helps them know that if you can do it and others can do it, they can too.

- **To encourage.** There are a multitude of things that can cause discouragement, even in the lives of mature believers. Christian leaders know well the value of giving encouragement on a regular basis. Telling stories of personal and corporate success lifts people's spirits.

When you contemplate sharing a personal story, use these four principles as a guide. They all facilitate the process of identification and will help leaders overcome real or perceived independence.

Independence is one of the few items on the short list of traits that are lethal to leaders. The underbelly of independence is pride, and if you do not work to submit your pride before God, your leadership will eventually erode to ineffectiveness. Independence repels people from you; identification draws them toward you.

Independence communicates, "I don't need you," and breeds more independence. When I consult with a church leader and sense an arrogant "just get out of my way and let me lead" sort of attitude, I know the same spirit has probably found its way into the congregation. Arrogance, which is rooted in pride, reproduces arrogance just as humility reproduces humility. It is not a mystery why congregations with independent leaders have teams full of independent volunteers. This atmosphere of independence often translates into pointless power struggles between otherwise good people. Good relationships and solid friendships are lost to independence, and leadership begins to quickly break down.

In contrast, identification cultivates interdependence. When people can identify with you, they are more likely to join you in fulfilling the mission of the church. A spirit of interdependence unites like-minded people and leverages the many different skills and resources they bring to the table.

LIGHTHEARTED VS. SERIOUS AND INTENSE

This is a relatively simple concept, but it is extremely important: lighten up. Life is serious enough without you making it more so. People don't easily connect with leaders who are overly intense. They want to laugh and see the lighter side of difficult situations. People need their leaders to bring life into dark situations and live out a spirit of optimism.

Leaders lift people up. This is a trait that has always marked my good friend Phil Stevenson. Phil and I went to high school together and laughed our way through four years of a German language class. We were on staff together at Skyline Wesleyan Church in San Diego, learned leadership from John Maxwell, and relaxed with our wives, Joni and Patti, while eating grilled peanut butter and jelly sandwiches. Phil always seems to be happy and in a great mood. In fact, he is usually laughing or beaming a great smile.

For the first several months after we met, I honestly wondered what Phil was on and wished he would share it with me. But after more than twenty-five years, I've learned that this is just who Phil is. He's a guy who sees the cup half full and finds the joy in every situation. This contributes in a significant way to the fact that he is a great leader. Today Phil is the director of church multiplication and leadership development for the Pacific-Southwest district of the Wesleyan Church. He has a passion for planting new churches and pours his heart into it through leadership development. Phil is serious about reaching people for Christ, but he makes the process fun for everyone involved. Leadership is a serious business, but it is possible to be serious about leadership without being down and gloomy as an individual. And there is a big difference between being intense about fulfilling the vision God has given you and being an intense person. No one wants to be around an intense person, but you must, at the right times, lead with intensity. If being lighthearted is difficult for you, start smiling more and look for the humor in every situation. Then pass that attitude on to others. You'll be amazed at the results.

Connecting with others is critical, but to truly develop strong relationships, leaders must go a step further. We must appreciate the people God gives us to lead. You may think this will be impossible to do with some people, but I assure you that's not the case. Read on and I'll show you how to truly value even the "difficult" people who come into your life.

Chapter Two

APPRECIATE PEOPLE FOR WHO THEY ARE

You must appreciate who a person is to discover who he can become.

DURING HIS PRESIDENCY, George W. Bush seemed to constantly face criticism. It began with his decision to go to war in Iraq and continued throughout his administration. He was accused of responding too slowly to the devastation Hurricane Katrina caused in New Orleans. He was criticized for his conservative Supreme Court nominations. And later he was blamed for the poor economy and rising gas prices.

At one point, it seemed as though every mainstream news report about President Bush was negative. The media's focus was completely on the Bush administration's flaws, and the president's approval rating hit an all-time low. The truth is, President Bush is an intelligent man who was under enormous pressure. I'm not suggesting he was flawless, but his potential and his personal value got buried under the rubble of the media's perceptions.

As leaders, we constantly run the risk of falling into the same trap. A good leader looks for the potential in a person and doesn't focus on his flaws. If we focus on a person's shortcomings, we'll never see him for who he can be, and the relationship will eventually break down. This is a simple concept but a very important one for a leader to grasp. You can't see a person clearly until you learn to appreciate him or her fully.

Appreciation is not toleration. When you tolerate someone (meaning you put up with or endure them), you dismiss that person

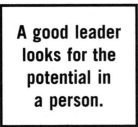

A good leader looks for the potential in a person.

as having little value to you or as someone who doesn't make a significant contribution. To appreciate a person (meaning you recognize his quality, significance, or magnitude, or admire him greatly), you must make an intentional effort to see the very best in that individual. In this context, appreciating someone is not saying thank you, though that is important. It is seeing the value, worth, and quality in that individual.

When I met Norwood Davis, I had nearly instant appreciation for who he was as a leader and a person. We ended up traveling together to Sri Lanka just a couple of weeks after the 2004 tsunami hit. For ten days I watched Norwood in action. He never complained but worked hard, was eager to help, loved the Sri Lankan people, and was quick to solve problems. It didn't take me long to see that Norwood was the kind of person I wanted on our staff. A couple of months later, Norwood joined the 12Stone team to help lead our global outreach and compassion ministries. It would have been a huge loss to our team had I focused on Norwood's weaknesses and overlooked his personal value and great leadership qualities. Our church would have missed out on the wonderful gifts God has given him.

You might be thinking, "Well, sure, it's easy to appreciate people when they're strong leaders like Norwood. You need to meet some of the people I'm around. They're a mess!" It's true that people are messy. They can have their own agendas and can cause problems in an organization. But if all you see when you look at people are the potential problems, you'll never appreciate them—and you will never see them as the reason you exist. As a leader, you have the opportunity to bring out a person's best and help him tap into his potential. The cool thing about this process is that you may see and appreciate someone's potential even before he does!

I hope you know what it's like to be appreciated for who you are. To be consistently appreciated by someone important to you, such as your boss, spouse, or a good friend, makes all the difference in the world. Think of how differently you respond to people who appreciate you compared with those who don't value what you have to offer. If you apply that feeling to the context of leadership, you'll quickly see how important it is to appreciate people.

Appreciation is an important skill that can be learned. So I want to take some time in this chapter to explain how we as leaders can strengthen our ability to truly value the people God puts in our lives.

ACCEPT PEOPLE THE WAY THEY ARE

Dave Ronne is the director of the redemptive arts team at 12Stone. He is responsible to lead, encourage, and organize a large number of filmmakers, technical directors, environmental design creators, musicians, songwriters, and other artists. Dave's leadership of this team is expected to result in an extraordinary weekend experience fifty-two times a year. This is no small feat. Sometimes it's like herding cats—it is difficult and can seem impossible. But Dave is a good leader, and he knows that if he wants an artist to perform like an artist, he can't force that person to behave like an engineer. He looks for the genius in each person and takes a pill to get over the rest.

Of course, Dave doesn't really take a pill when he gets frustrated. He doesn't have to. People love being on his team, and they willingly go the distance for him. Why? Because when people know a leader loves and accepts them the way they are, they allow themselves to be stretched to become all they can become.

Accepting people the way they are is difficult for most leaders because they want to help people grow and realize their potential. This is a positive and potentially productive tension of leadership that will always exist. Leaders are also under pressure to get things done. However, before we can help people grow or get anything done, we need to connect with people and accept them as they are. If we don't do this, we'll end up doing everything ourselves because we won't be developing new leaders. It may seem easier to do things by yourself, but it's not smart. You can't get much accomplished that way, and you'll miss out on the fun of developing leaders.

I have found that when I focus on looking for the potential in people, it's easy to accept them as they are. It's all about perspective. Some leaders see potential when they look at the people around them, and some see problems. Admittedly, for leaders who are overworked, looking for the potential in people represents more work, so they tend to see the problems. These leaders aren't necessarily problem-oriented leaders, but when they see a person's problems, it's easier for them to shut that individual down than to expend the energy required to develop him into a potential leader.

Leadership overload is a reality, but the answer isn't to avoid new sources of potential leadership. The answer is to cut other obligations out of your to-do list and start looking for the potential in people. This isn't easy, but it's a must.

John Maxwell is a bottom-line leader. He thinks fast and moves quickly. My leadership style is more process-oriented, and I, therefore, take more time to lead through certain issues. This could be seen as a problem by some experienced and heavily burdened leaders. John, however, mined my potential, cultivated my gifts, forgave my mistakes, and fanned the flame of leadership within me. Years of experience have caused me to move much faster within my process-orientation style. In those early years, if John had focused on speed rather than results, he may never have seen my potential. Instead, he gave me room to be myself. And in time I produced results that surprised both of us.

How are you doing in this area? Are you generally open toward people and accepting of them, or is your first response one of distrust or even cynicism? When you meet someone new, is your first instinct to question his motives or to enjoy his personality? As you get to know someone, do you intuitively give him the benefit of the doubt or wonder why he does things a particular way? When someone offends you, are you quick to forgive or do you write the person off? Your answers to these questions will help you get a handle on how accepting you are of people. The more you are able to embrace people as they are, the easier it will be for you to see their potential. Keep these questions in mind so you will stay focused on the importance of relationships in your leadership!

Value People as Part of God's Creation

When someone cuts me off on the highway, my first thought isn't that they are part of God's creation. My first thought is, *why* are they part of creation? Despite my frustrations, those individuals *are* part of God's handiwork, and they deserve to be treated with respect. Genesis 1 tells us after God created mankind, He considered everything He made "very good" (v. 31).

Valuing human beings is more than merely the decent and moral thing to do; it is God-honoring. Creation is the expression of God's hand in our midst. When we disrespect creation, we disrespect God Himself. I don't mean this in a radical way. I'm not above stomping a spider, swatting a mosquito, or cutting down trees to build houses. But God formed people in His own image (Gen. 1:27). The psalmist David declared that we are "fearfully and wonderfully made" (Ps. 139:14). As leaders we would be wise to follow the heart of David and acknowledge the beauty of God's creation in all people, even when it's not easy.

I can't address this point without touching on the importance of having the right attitude. A leader's attitude is like oxygen to the body. If the body is filled with a poison such as carbon monoxide, it won't last long. Likewise, if your attitude gets sour, your leadership will head south in a hurry. Your attitude shapes how you see people and life in general. I love the story of the man who fell from a fifteen-story building. Someone yelled out of a seventh-story window, "Are you OK?" And the falling man yelled back, "So far so good!" Now that is a positive attitude!

As a leader you are required to have a good attitude—though it should be more realistic than that of the man falling from the fifteenth floor. A good attitude doesn't ignore reality; it seeks to make the best of it. A good attitude turns problems into opportunities. A leader with a good attitude brings hope from discouragement.

A pastor called me once to discuss a situation involving a person who had recently gotten married. This person was a believer who married an unbeliever. The pastor didn't believe this was biblically correct or wise, but he said, "Well, Dan, maybe she'll lead him to the Lord. Let's pray for that." That is a positive attitude. This pastor would never recommend that a Christian marry someone who didn't share his or her faith. But because this couple ignored this advice and was already married, he hoped to see good come from it.

Believe it or not, a leader's attitude isn't everything. Attitude goes a long way, but it also helps when leaders actually like people. Too many leaders profess to love people as God does, but then they behave as though they don't like the individuals they serve. People know when they're liked, no matter what we say. I know people can, on occasion, be irritating. But the right response is to extend a full measure of grace to them.

If you find people more of an interruption than a blessing, you might be a candidate for a new perspective. If you see people as "more work" rather than a privilege to serve, you may need some rest. You may need to remind yourself that Jesus gave His life for the people following you. That's guaranteed to produce an attitude adjustment!

I like people. Personality quirks make them interesting and fun to me. The individuals I interact with know I like them, and the ones you interact with know if you like them or not as well. God created every person with worth and purpose. Make it your mission to discover the worth and purpose of every person God puts in your path. Make it a habit to value and esteem everyone you meet.

When you do so, you honor God and are likely to establish a wonderful new relationship.

BECOME A STUDENT OF HUMAN NATURE

What makes driven people so driven? What causes carefree people to be carefree? Why are highly productive people so productive? Leaders study these kinds of questions carefully. They don't do this only in the office with their colleagues. They get involved in the lives of the people they lead. This is how human nature is meant to be studied—not from an ivory tower but among real people in real life. Part of being a good leader is knowing what makes people tick.

After I completed my undergraduate degree in criminal justice administration and before I went to Asbury Theological Seminary, I spent some time working as a private investigator. I'm certain I know God's purpose for leading me down that path, even if for a season. Had I gone straight from college to seminary and then immediately into a church, I would have been one naive young pastor. My brief career as a PI gave me immensely helpful insight into human nature.

One case I worked involved a teenage girl from an upper-middle-class home. The girl suffered several shallow stab wounds in her abdomen, and we were assigned to protect her and find whoever did this. It's a long and sad story, so let me fast-forward to the end. The wounds were self-inflicted. It didn't matter that she lived in a beautiful home and her parents made lots of money. It didn't matter that she was bright and popular. What mattered was that her career-focused parents were never home, and she was desperate for their attention.

A solid grasp of human nature will help you quickly understand why people behave the way they do. You will lead better when you realize that hurting people hurt people, insecure people need attention and reassurance, and healthy people want to help people. When you know that everyone wants to be on a winning team, to make their life count, and to love and be loved, you can interpret what they say and do more accurately.

People lash out when they are under pressure or backed into a corner. And when someone's response far outweighs the situation at hand, that usually means something struck a raw nerve or the person has something weighing on him. Books could be filled with nothing but observations about human nature. In fact, it would be a great learning experience for you to write down as many facts about human nature as you can think of. As you make new observations, you can update the list and use it as your own personal reference guide for understanding and responding to people.

So how do you gain wisdom about human nature? You don't need a PhD in psychology to be a good leader. Developing a few simple habits will provide all the knowledge you need to understand what makes people tick.

- *Pay attention to people.* This first step is the easiest. Did you ever have a teacher or a coach tell you to pay attention? My reason for encouraging you to do this is the same. You'll never realize how much information you're missing until you become aware of what's going on around you.

- *Keep your head in the game.* This takes effort. To understand human nature, you must have enough self-discipline to keep from focusing on yourself and invest significant energy into others. You must be self-aware but not self-absorbed.

- *Ask meaningful questions.* Small talk is a good social skill, but the ability to ask the right questions at the right time is far more important. Find a way to make all your lengthy conversations purposeful.

- *Learn to read between the lines.* Human behavior is generally both innocent and complicated. This is true because at some level we are all broken people. Sin is part of the world. Christ can mend our wounds, but He doesn't remove us from the world. Human nature is, at its best, imperfect. This can become frustrating, but as leaders we can't focus only on people's actions. We must look deeper to see their needs.

- *Genuinely care.* It's amazing how much people will trust you and open up when they know you truly care about them. Showing genuine concern for people will not only help you understand human nature, but it also will create some wonderful ministry opportunities.

As you become a student of human nature, you will find yourself amazed and frustrated. People are complicated, and the more you learn about human behavior, the more tempting it will be for you to become cynical. But few things will derail your effectiveness as a leader faster. The best way to prevent cynicism from creeping in is to pour your energies into doing what is in the best interest of each individual you serve and commit to helping them live a better life.

Move Toward "Difficult" People

It is counterintuitive to move toward difficult people. It's like putting your hand on a hot stove, pulling it off, and putting it right back on again. It doesn't make sense. But if you really want to increase your ability to appreciate people, you must learn to value difficult people too. Jesus addressed this in the Sermon on the Mount. He said, "If you love those who love you, what reward will you get? Are not even the tax collectors doing that? And if you greet only your brothers, what are you doing more than others? Do not even pagans do that?" (Matt. 5:46-47).

Jesus was speaking about loving your enemies, but the principle applies well to accepting difficult people. It's easy to love and accept your friends, fans, and followers. The real challenge is learning how to appreciate those who test you. If someone is hard to get along with, ask yourself why. What needs does he have? What hurts does she feel? What pressures is he under? Like in the children's story about the brave mouse that removed the thorn from a lion's paw, if you'll take a risk and get close enough to that difficult person to show him some compassion, you'll often discover an amazing individual beneath the surface.

Keep in mind that being different isn't a bad thing. The church and its leaders have, at times, been guilty of not appreciating or accepting people who veer from the mainstream. This is seen in a number of areas—from style of worship to clothing choices to doctrine and theology. I know of a person who was asked to leave a church in Boston because he raised his hands in worship. One couple who now attend 12Stone said their former church required men to wear coats and ties and women to wear dresses. If someone didn't comply with the "dress code," they were overlooked for leadership opportunities.

I recently spoke with a man who struggled with the fact that his church permits women to hold leadership positions. I tried to help him see the biblical basis for this and the value of having women leading in the church. I don't know that I changed his mind, but that wasn't the point. I wanted to help him see that "different" wasn't automatically wrong and that he could easily serve alongside people who didn't share his views.

This example illustrates another important point. Disagreement doesn't necessarily indicate that a person is a troublemaker. Meetings can get intense when someone strongly disagrees with an issue the leader is passionate about. Church budget meetings are notorious for producing "heat in the kitchen," but this happens in dozens of ways within ministries. Perhaps a pastor presents the need to hire a children's pastor, but the majority not only opposes him, they also insist the money would be better spent feeding the poor. Or maybe a leader thinks it's time to sell the building and relocate, but a group of influential board members doesn't want to move and thinks the ministry should renovate and expand the current facility.

The list of possible conflicts is endless, but the bottom line is the same. A person shouldn't be labeled a problem just because he disagrees with the leader. If you want to truly appreciate people, don't avoid the ones who challenge you. In fact, those individuals are often leaders waiting to be discovered. One of my favorite ministry stories is about a person who, year after year, asked annoying and often petty questions about the church's financial position at the annual business meeting. Finally, the pastor invited the individual to become the church treasurer. (I don't recommend this move.) In this case, it was the pastor's wife, and the annual business meetings ran fine after that. How things went at home, none of us will ever know.

LOOK FOR THE BEST IN PEOPLE

More often than not you find what you look for. This is true in day-to-day life and with people. If you look for flaws in a situation, you find them; if you look for a person's best, you find it.

In 1987 God prompted me to begin something I call Joshua's Men. It's a yearlong mentoring process during which small groups of men meet together to study a variety of subjects related to leadership. Almost twenty-five years later, Joshua's Men continues to be one of the highlights of my life. I've watched many of the men I mentored develop into phenomenal leaders who are now leading Joshua's Men groups of their own. But in the early days, I was the only one mentoring the guys.

I met monthly with my Joshua's Men group, and I poured all I could into each person. My goal was to see the guys become better leaders in their homes, churches, and workplaces, and for each of them to have a better quality life. One of the coolest experiences for me was watching the guys in Joshua's Men begin to mentor one another as the year progressed.

> **You find what you look for. If you look for flaws, you find them; if you look for a person's best, you find it.**

In order for me to lead a successful Joshua's Men group, I had to look for the best in the guys participating. I found that when I consistently sought the best in each man, that set a tone for the year. The playing field was built around my desire to see the men succeed, and that passion was evident from the initial selection of the guys to the individual moments of encouragement, challenge, and coaching I had with them.

This didn't guarantee success, but it increased the potential for it exponentially. I have lost count of how many men have asked me, "Why did you select me to be in Joshua's Men?" Though the specifics were different, each time I told them it was because I saw something special—a spark, something unique about them, something God could use. This set the stage for me to nurture the best in each man. The more I looked for the best in these men, the more I found it and the more I was able to appreciate each man as a person. Today I am blessed to mentor men who are leading Joshua's Men groups. It is a profound privilege to watch the *Amplified Leadership* process at work as I develop leaders who in turn are developing other leaders.

I know the power of looking for the best in people because that has been done for me. For years I took guitar lessons with a man named Joe Carpenter. For all my enthusiasm, I wasn't the strongest guitar player who ever lived. I would typically stumble through songs or fail to remember the notes on the scale. I usually had some kind of misstep. Although learning to play guitar definitely wasn't smooth sailing for me, Joe always found something good to say about my playing. And trust me, he had to look long and hard to find it.

Joe died unexpectedly in 2005, and I still think of him often and miss the time we spent together. I miss his sense of humor. He would often say to me, "Don't quit your day job." Or, "I hope you're a *really* good preacher." We both knew I wasn't the most skilled guitarist. Joe kept it light but real. But if he thought I was getting discouraged, he would say, "Dan, do you have fun when you play?" And I would tell him that I loved it. Then Joe would reply, "That's all that really matters. Keep on pickin' 'cause you're doing just fine."

I will never be a great guitar player. But because Joe looked for the best and invested in me, I was able to teach my son, John-Peter, to play guitar. Unlike his father, John-Peter has tremendous potential to become a great guitarist. As I listen to him play, I'm still following Joe's lead. I look for the best in my son and cheer him on. And when he gets stuck, I ask him if he's having fun. If he is, I tell him to keep on pickin' because he's doing just fine.

Establishing great relationships is the foundation of *Amplified Leadership,* but as you can see from the illustration below, the process doesn't end there. You can't be a leader if no one is following you. Read on and I'll explain how to turn those new relationships into engaged followers.

AMPLIFY YOUR LEADERSHIP

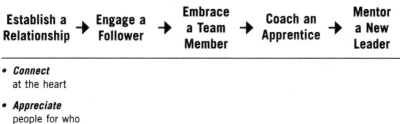

Establish a Relationship	→	Engage a Follower	→	Embrace a Team Member	→	Coach an Apprentice	→	Mentor a New Leader

- *Connect*
  at the heart

- *Appreciate*
  people for who
  they are

PART

TWO

ENGAGE A FOLLOWER

You aren't a leader if no one is following you.

JESUS ENGAGED HIS disciples Simon, Andrew, James, and John with just two words. He said, "Follow me." And they did (Mark 1:16–20). If only twenty-first-century leadership worked that way.

Jesus's group of disciples quickly grew to twelve, and on the Day of Pentecost the number had risen to one hundred twenty. By the time the apostle Paul emerged on the scene, Jesus's followers numbered in the thousands. In the centuries since then, millions have chosen to follow Christ through the challenge of leaders like you. Challenging people to follow Christ is our mission, but as leaders, we must also get people to follow us. This simple and simultaneously complex act will always be the evidence of our leadership.

John Maxwell is well known for saying, "He who thinketh he leadeth but hath no one following is only taking a walk!" I've known this principle for nearly thirty years. Yet the longer I lead, and the more I understand the depth of leadership, the stronger my grasp of this truth becomes. Author James MacGregor Burns discusses this in his Pulitzer Prize–winning book *Leadership*. He writes, "Much of what passes as leadership—conspicuous position-taking without followers or follow through, posturing on various public stages, manipulation without general purpose, authoritarianism—is no more leadership than the behavior of small boys marching in front of a parade, who continue to strut along main street after the procession has turned down a side street toward the fairgrounds."[1] The fact that people follow you doesn't mean you are a *good* leader; it simply means you *can* lead. Effective leadership involves much more. Good leaders must be good followers.

It is impossible to overestimate the powerful example you will set by submitting to authority. Whether it's following a decision from the church board, your immediate supervisor, or a word from God, your ability to follow cheerfully and with a servant's heart will not go unnoticed. What's more, the act of following creates the right attitude within a leader, an attitude that earns him the privilege of leading others. It is the very attitude Jesus modeled and that the apostle Paul challenged His followers to imitate.

> Do nothing out of selfish ambition or vain conceit, but in humility consider others better than yourselves. Each of you should look not only to your own interests, but also to the interests of others. Your attitude should be the same as that of Christ Jesus: Who, being in very nature God, did not consider equality with God something to be grasped, but made himself nothing, taking the very nature of a servant, being

made in human likeness. And being found in appearance as
a man, he humbled himself and became obedient to death—
even death on a cross!

—PHILIPPIANS 2:3-8

There are several reasons a person must to learn to submit to
others in a spirit of servanthood to qualify for spiritual leadership.
Submission prevents a spirit of rebellion, a spirit of arrogance, and
a spirit of independence. Each of those spirits is rooted in pride—
and pride is the end of all leaders. Having the attitude of Christ will
help us remain humble and fit for leadership.

STRONG LEADERS KNOW HOW TO FOLLOW

Following someone or something is an intentional act. No one follows by accident. Although people need and want leadership, following a leader is not a natural human bent. Our nature is to go
our own way. When we follow, it's only because we have chosen to
do so.

Kevin Myers is the senior pastor at 12Stone Church, where I
serve as executive pastor. Although I am also in a position of leadership, I submit to Kevin. There are a number of good reasons for
this. God has granted us an ordained partnership. Kevin is a gifted
leader whom I respect. He's smart and intuitive, and he is committed to listening to and obeying God's voice. Kevin has many
qualities that make it easy for me to submit to him, but ultimately I
follow him because I *choose* to. I am no different from anyone else.

If someone follows you, it's because he chooses to do so also.
No matter what qualities you bring to the table, people will always
make a choice to submit to your leadership, and this is all the more
true for volunteers. Remember, if a person chooses to follow you,

he can choose to *stop* following you as well! You may have the authority as the leader, but the people ultimately have the power. They demonstrate their power of choice every time they support the ministry with their wallets and their feet.

Every check they write, service they attend, or activity they support is a sobering reminder of this reality. You may choose to see these acts as a reflection of a person's spiritual maturity, but that is a limited view. You are the leader. Each individual is responsible for his or her maturity, but you are a chief influence to that end. Much like a parent, you as a ministry leader affect how the person "grows up" in his faith.

Winning people's trust in our leadership is not a one-time deal. We must continue to earn people's loyal following throughout our time as leaders. Likewise, leaders never outgrow the need to follow. A willingness to follow isn't something leaders demonstrate only when they're young and inexperienced.

One of our board members is a successful businesswoman named Cynthia Kaye. She owns a company and brings great wisdom to our team (while managing to keep us all laughing). She and her husband, Ron, have demonstrated great entrepreneurial leadership through the years. Cynthia oversees a huge staff and is used to calling the shots. Yet her maturity allows her to also be a good follower as she serves on the board. She presents suggestions but recognizes that she must submit to the other leaders within the board.

This is a sign of great leadership. Good leaders understand that a person's authority, experience, or accomplishments will never exempt him from the need to follow and remain accountable to others. And good leaders never take followers for granted. Whether you are responsible for a small group or a large congregation, you must remember that every person—every follower—possesses great significance and must be treated accordingly. As we examine the second practice of *Amplified Leadership*, engaging a follower, you may find it helpful to keep the following thoughts in mind.

1. Followers want significance even more than they want success.

Everyone wants to be on a winning team, but more importantly, they want to be on a team that genuinely makes a difference. Don't waste people's time. It's your responsibility as the leader to do more than merely keep people busy with activities. You must provide opportunities for meaningful engagement within the vision God has given you. It's true that what constitutes meaning is subjective, but the purpose of ministry is not. It's summed up in one question: Are people's lives being changed? This will always be the bottom line for spiritual leaders.

When 12Stone's leadership team called for volunteers to join a relief force for Hurricane Katrina victims, hundreds of people quickly came forward. They knew this cause mattered. People needed help, and by serving they would make a difference. This kind of engagement that propels the ministry's vision is far more meaningful to people than serving on a committee that does little to connect them with a bigger purpose.

2. Followers want to know you have their best interest at heart.

When my wife, Patti, and I moved to Atlanta from California, we attended North Point Community Church, where Andy Stanley is the pastor. North Point is a huge church, and I didn't know Andy at all when we first started attending. I didn't know if he genuinely cared about people, though I assumed he did. After a couple of opportunities to get to know Andy, I quickly saw that he did indeed care.

I was given the opportunity to serve on his board of elders, and I saw that even behind the scenes Andy was the real deal. Not only is he a brilliant leader and a gifted communicator, but he also genuinely loves people. It's easy to follow someone like that, and we did. Patti and I co-led an area fellowship and a small group in complete alignment with Andy's vision, and we had a blast doing it. Patti modeled the same heart for people as part of North Point's parents' ministry, KidStuf. She affectionately became known as a "bag lady" because of her commitment to welcome first-time visitors with goodie bags.

3. Followers always pay a price.

A leader is obligated to live a life worthy of the price followers pay. Again, Jesus set the pace for us. When He called the early disciples to follow Him, He asked a lot of them. They left their jobs and the people they knew and loved, and ultimately they gave their lives for their faith. When we ask people to trust our leadership and follow Christ, we ask no less. We may not literally ask them to give their physical lives, but we do ask them to die to themselves and live a new life in Christ. This is no small request. As a leader, I want the investment I make in people's lives to be worthy of the price they pay to follow me.

LEARNING TO DANCE

For years, Patti wanted me to take ballroom dance lessons with her. I knew this would be painful, but I finally gave in. We learned the foxtrot, tango, waltz, rumba, and other dances. In truth, Patti learned those dances, and I tried not to hurt myself. It didn't take long for both of us to realize that if we were to be successful dancers, one of us had to lead and the other had to follow—intentionally and willingly. And neither of us had the easier job.

Of all the hobbies I've ever taken up, ballroom dancing was the clearest example of the reciprocal nature of leadership I've ever encountered. A good leader paired with a bad follower will look like a train wreck on the dance floor. And a good follower paired with a bad leader will experience just as much chaos. Both parties have to work in harmony for the dance to be enjoyable. The same is true in leadership. It takes two—an encouraging leader and an inspired follower—to create a beautiful and breathtaking dance. When they are done correctly, encouragement and inspiration work together beautifully to engage followers. If you are ready to dance, read on.

Chapter Three

ENCOURAGE PEOPLE TO BUILD THEM UP

*Leaders who build up those they influence bring out
the best in them, so people want to follow.*

ENCOURAGEMENT IS A kind of fuel. It enables people to try harder, reach farther, dig deeper, and hold on longer than they previously thought possible. Leadership without encouragement is like running without shoes. You can do it, but it doesn't feel good, and you won't last long. When vision is detached from encouragement, it comes across as drudgery rather than a dream, a problem rather than a privilege, and a job rather than a joy. If a leader truly wants to engage a follower, he must practice the intentional and consistent art of encouragement. This is nonnegotiable.

I've never met anyone who received too much encouragement. In nearly three decades of ministry leadership, during which I have traveled to well over one hundred churches and talked with thousands of ministry leaders, I've never heard of anyone quitting because he or she was overencouraged. In contrast, the number one reason people throw in the towel is because they did not receive enough encouragement. John Maxwell has said, "Encouragement is 51 percent of successful leadership." I believe that. Without this leadership lifeblood, even the most inspiring vision won't take hold in people's hearts.

Encouragement is a core component of hope. It helps people believe they can have and contribute to a better future. It bolsters their courage when they would otherwise shrink back. It builds their confidence to do things they never thought they could accomplish. When my son, John-Peter, was about four years old, I took him to swim in a pool. I wanted him to jump in the water, but he would have nothing to do with it. He just stood there on the edge of the pool. So I got in the pool and assured him that he could do it, that it would be fun, and that I would catch him right after he hit the water. In he jumped, and he's been diving in on his own ever since.

This is the power of encouragement in action, and it makes just as big a difference as we get older. When I was a student at San Diego State University, I served as a leader within the college ministry at Skyline Wesleyan Church. I loved the local church, but pastoral leadership was the furthest thing from my mind. Then something profound happened. The late Orval Butcher, Skyline's founding pastor, told me he believed in me. Pastor Butcher said he saw leadership gifts in me and sensed that God might be calling me into full-time ministry.

At first I thought he was nuts. But his sincere, loving, and enthusiastic encouragement persisted, and I began to believe it too. This allowed me to be receptive to God's voice and hear my calling to ministry personally. Without that encouragement I might still be working as a private investigator, my first job out of college.

I once heard Rick Warren talk about Saddleback Church's challenging beginnings. In its first fifteen years, the church changed locations nearly eighty times! Rick laughed when he said there were some weeks when people had to check the newspaper to see where the church was meeting for worship that Sunday. He was having even more fun when he said there were some people they hid the newspaper from!

During those trying early years, Rick said the congregation lost about $100,000 on a land deal when they were trying to find a permanent location. What a blow. It was a difficult loss to take. But the congregation didn't let that stop them. They took a deep breath and kept going, and eventually secured a better land deal.[1] The church was able to keep moving forward because Rick had been investing encouragement into his congregation from day one. He communicates hope and helps people believe there will be a better future.

Traits of Encouraging Leaders

Are you an encouraging leader? Some people have a gift for exhortation and find it natural to encourage others. But most of us can improve in this area. In this chapter I will list several traits I have found in leaders who successfully encourage their followers, as well as some of the important reasons it is vital that ministry leaders develop this skill.

Encouraging leaders naturally draw people to them.

Every morning when I wake up, I thank God for all the incredible opportunities He has packed into the day. I honestly believe I will have a meaningful, productive, and enjoyable day. But I know that as wonderful as life is, it is also difficult. Each day brings potential pressures related to finances, health, relationships—the list goes on and on. The certainty of difficult times in life can and will weigh people down.

> **If you are an encouraging leader, people will gravitate toward you.**

Discouragement is a reality of life, and people need to be lifted up. Encouragement is not a simple art practiced mostly by soft and unproductive leaders. Far from it. The ability to encourage is actually one of the true tests of leadership. If you are an encouraging leader, people will gravitate toward you. If, for instance, you hold a recognized leadership position in a local church, people should stop you in the lobby after service or at the local restaurant where church members tend to gather. If you're not being stopped, something is wrong because people are naturally drawn to leaders who build them up.

Please don't get hung up on numbers. It doesn't matter whether three people or thirty-three people seek you out after the service. And being an encourager is not about having a larger-than-life personality. God designed your personality just the way He wanted it. You don't have to be the loud person at the party who is wearing the lamp shade as a hat to be an encouraging leader. What is important is that people enjoy being around you because you make them feel better about themselves and life in general.

I'm sure you can think of people you love being around. When you see them, you instinctively smile and begin to move in their direction. I am fortunate to have many people in my life like that. Dave Bearchell is one of them. Dave is an elder on 12Stone's church board and a true prayer warrior. In fact, he is affectionately known as "Prayer Boy." We say this with honor and, I must admit, to rib him a little bit. Dave always has a positive, faith-filled perspective on any situation. And he has a quick smile, a great (dry) sense of humor, and a warm heart for everyone he connects with. When I see Dave, life is better.

What do people tend to say about you? You may not be exactly like Dave, but you don't want to be the opposite kind of person either—someone whose motto seems to be "life is hard and then you die." You know how people like that make you feel. When you see them, you want to run because they will suck the life out of you.

If you are a leader in a local church and people don't move toward you, there is a reason. Ask someone who loves you to be honest with you. Ask him or her to help you discover why people aren't drawn to you. I'm not suggesting that something is psychologically or spiritually wrong with you. Being a good encourager is a skill that can be learned and developed. The challenge is that until you learn to be an encourager (evidenced by people wanting to be around you), you will have difficulty leading to your potential—and in some cases, leading at all.

The problem might be something simple. Many years ago someone walked up to me and asked if I was mad. I said, "No, why do you ask that?" The person said, "Because you are frowning and look like you are mad or something." That little exchange was of immense help to me. My natural and comfortable facial expression doesn't look much like Ronald McDonald's happy face! So I've learned to let my heart show through my smile. It may be more complicated than that for you. Perhaps you have a negative view of life or people. Whatever the case, I urge you to confront the issue. The importance of being a great encourager can't be overstated.

If you think your ability to encourage needs improvement, allow me to offer some advice that will point you in the right direction. If people don't come to you, go to them. Don't be bashful. Just walk right up to them and share a few words that will lift them up and give them a sense of hope.

Encouraging leaders communicate with a positive bias.

The art of encouragement doesn't have to be complicated. Sometimes all you need to do is make someone laugh. The key is to avoid any impulse to communicate something negative. Don't talk about how tired you are, how much work you have to do, how bad the traffic is, the price of gas, how miserable the weather is, or how much your back hurts. Be a light in that person's day.

Being a positive person is essential to effective and sustained leadership, but I realize that everyone has bad days. When you hit a rough patch, take a break. Talk with a trusted friend, and open your heart. Tell it like you feel it. Kick and scream if you need to, but do your best to quickly move past the issue and continue leading.

You may need more than a cup of coffee with a friend. You may need to connect with a counselor for a season. That's OK. It's better for you to confront the problem than allow it to hinder your effectiveness as a leader. Our primary disposition among the people we lead cannot be negative. We must live in a way that causes people to be drawn toward us and lifted up.

Having a positive disposition doesn't mean you are clueless about the pressures of life. It means you are a smart leader who understands that people have enough stuff pulling them down and they need you to lift them up. I also don't mean to suggest that having a positive bias means you never have difficult conversations with people. In fact, it's quite the opposite. Good leaders are not afraid to confront important issues. But the reception to those difficult talks is usually more positive when the leader is known to be an encouraging, positive, and uplifting person.

It also helps to always be sincere in what you say. The apostle Paul reminds us of this in Ephesians 4:29: "Do not let any unwholesome talk come out of your mouths, but only what is helpful for building others up according to their needs, that it may benefit those who listen." Sincerity communicates love and concern and ultimately builds people up.

John Maxwell is the most positive person I know. He has great faith in people and sees life for its potential instead of its problems. He's not delusional, though. John knows that life can be difficult. He just refuses to get stuck there. We were in Israel in 2010 just a few months after John had knee surgery. During the trip, John began to experience pain in his knee, and climbing all the hills and steps from Masada to Jerusalem became a challenge. But he never let his pain keep him from giving great leadership. He served people, baptized dozens in the Jordan River, and created a fun atmosphere throughout the trip. Even after knowing John for so many years, I've rarely heard him complain. That's the way it is with encouraging leaders. They communicate with a positive bias.

Kevin Queen is another leader who exudes encouragement. As pastor of 12Stone Church's Hamilton Mill campus in suburban Atlanta, Kevin is a gifted communicator whose preaching always leaves people feeling uplifted. This attribute is part of what makes him such a great leader both on and off the platform. People want to follow leaders like Kevin—leaders who are positive.

I encourage you to take some time to assess your own level of positivity. Would people describe you as a positive person? Do you consistently have a positive attitude toward people and life in general? If the answer to either of those questions is no, the effectiveness of your leadership could be in jeopardy.

Encouraging leaders are quick to invest generously in others.

Steve Poe and Corey Baker aren't on staff at 12Stone Church, but you wouldn't know it from the level of influence they have. For the last several years Steve and Corey have each been mentoring groups of seven or eight guys through our Joshua's Men leadership program. "J-Men," as the guys call it, started with a vision to see men give their talent and energy to become spiritual leaders in their homes, workplaces, and church. Today the program is seeing amazing results. The curriculum we use plays a part, but the real secret to its success is the investment the leaders make in each group of men.

Steve and Corey are busy husbands, fathers, and businessmen, and Joshua's Men is no small commitment. The yearlong experience includes monthly meetings, time with prayer partners, retreats, assigned reading, leadership lessons, unique projects, and considerable time for mentoring. Yet I've never heard Steve or Corey complain. They clearly love pouring themselves into these guys, and the results speak for themselves. Dozens of men at 12Stone speak often of the transformation they experienced because of the encouraging and challenging leadership they received from Steve and Corey.

Steve and Corey want to see a return on their investment of time, but they give to the men they mentor with no strings attached. This is the mark of a good leader, though it can be a fine line to walk. Leaders can't afford to invest their time in someone and not see evidence of growth. Yet the process of cultivating new leaders is much more organic than mechanical. Sometimes I'm tempted to encourage leaders to erase all the lines and strategies and just go with the flow, but that ultimately wouldn't be very helpful. There must be benchmarks of progress. A leader's time is valuable and can't be wasted or lost.

The way to balance this tension is to focus on the person first and the results second. This may lead you to make some tough decisions. If it becomes obvious that you are working harder than the person you're mentoring, you may choose to stop investing in the individual. I challenge you not to make this decision lightly. Even in situations like these, I would encourage you to stay with the individual a little longer than you may think necessary. Give him the benefit of the doubt, and do everything possible to help him before you cut him loose. When a leader embraces this attitude, he often will begin to see the desired results.

I love telling a story about Keith Drury, who is one of my mentors and encouragers. Keith is a professor in the ministry department at Indiana Wesleyan University. They call him "Coach D." When I was a young and thin leader with lots of dark brown hair (my, how things change), Keith demonstrated such generosity that it marked my life for good.

I was clueless in ministry, and Keith was mentoring a group of us young guys he called The Cadre. I didn't have any money, and Keith knew that, but he believed I would benefit from a cool leadership conference that was coming up. After we met one day, Keith showed me a good book to read and stuffed it in my briefcase. When I later opened it, I found two one-hundred-dollar bills stapled inside with a note that said, "I believe in you, and I'll see you at the conference." I was blown away. Two hundred dollars is a lot of money now, but it was a ton of money back then! Yet what was even more valuable than the money was the time and encouragement Keith gave me. His investment is paying dividends even to this day!

Who are you investing in? Are your efforts intentional? Do you see results? Your process doesn't need to be sophisticated, and it shouldn't be complicated. In fact, it will probably be better if it isn't. It's amazing how much can be accomplished over a cup of coffee.

It doesn't matter whether you're pouring your life into five or twenty or dozens of people. The specific number isn't what counts. The important thing is that you invest in others. There's nothing like it. Give more than you expect back and watch what happens!

Encouraging leaders are grateful for what they have.

It's difficult to consistently encourage others when you are focused on what you don't have rather than what you do have. Any of us can easily slide into this mode. But when we play the comparison game, we will eventually lose because there is always someone who has more. We all know people who have a bigger house, newer car, more money, a larger church. You can make the list as personal as you want. There will always be someone with cooler friends, more successful kids, a slimmer waistline, better hair—trust me, it never ends.

It's important that we appreciate what we have. This is probably not a revelation to you, but it's easy to forget. I thank God every day for all He's blessed me with. The list of things to be grateful for is so long, if I really give thanks I don't have time to complain about anything. Only when I take my eyes off all I have and begin to compare myself with others do I lose my sense of gratitude. Here's the key. What's important is not how much we own but how we view what we have. There are wealthy people who have more material things than a dozen people would ever own, yet they don't appreciate them. Meanwhile, there are people with comparatively little who are genuinely grateful. Contentment is wrapped up in how you see things.

Grateful people have a special way of viewing life. They find joy in the simple things—a cup of coffee with a good friend, a perfect day on the beach, the laughter of their children, or a new family who decided to visit church on Sunday. It's a lens from which they embrace the good in their life. This perspective profoundly affects leadership. It helps leaders become more generous, positive, joyful, creative, and energetic. People want to be around them, and a sort of personal momentum begins to gain traction in their lives. This momentum gives leaders a natural inclination to encourage others.

Would those you lead describe you as a grateful person? Can they feel your gratitude toward them? Does your family see you as a grateful person? If you answered yes to these questions, then great. You are ahead of the game, and I'm confident your leadership reflects your grateful spirit and encouraging words.

If you struggle with gratitude, hang in there. You're not alone. Many leaders have a difficult time with this, but there are some practical ways to cultivate a grateful heart. First, stop comparing. As I mentioned before, if you compare yourself with others, eventually you will come up short. Second, be careful about buying into the cultural lie that you deserve more. God didn't promise you more; He promised to take care of your needs. Third, make a daily practice of thanking God for your friends and family, gifts and abilities, church and possessions. You won't have time to cover all of this every day, and that in itself will help you become grateful!

I can assure you that people are much quicker to follow a

leader with a grateful outlook on life than someone who demon-strates, even subtly, an unappreciative spirit. As an added bonus, having a grateful perspective will increase your joy immeasurably. It would be a shame for you to miss the joy in this journey through life. A grateful heart will enable you to truly enjoy the ride!

> **Your main job is not to grow a specific ministry in your church, or even the church overall. It is to grow people.**

One of the things I love most are the simple notes my kids write in my birthday cards. There's just nothing like hearing them express gratitude for who I am as their dad. It warms my heart and makes me want to be a better dad. Gratitude will have the same kind of impact on those you lead. It will cultivate encouragement more than you can imagine.

Encouraging leaders know the value of spiritual encouragement.

If you ever want an example of a true spiritual encourager, look no further than Barnabas. In Acts 11, the Bible says Barnabas intentionally looked for evidence of grace and encouraged the people to continue their spiritual progress and remain committed in their faith (vv. 19-24). Barnabas passionately wanted to know that people were pursuing maturity in Christ. He cared not only about their eternity but also about the current condition of their hearts.

Perhaps it goes without saying, but encouraging people in their faith is at the very epicenter of your role as a spiritual leader. Your main job is not to grow a specific ministry in your church, or even the church overall. It is to grow people. When this happens, your church moves forward, and the kingdom of God advances!

Doug and Sherry Bennett are great friends of mine and productive leaders. They are positive people who invest deeply in others. But something has consistently stood out with them. They take spiritual encouragement to the next level. A little more than fifteen years ago they took their own time, and dime, and flew to San Diego to meet with me. I will never forget this encounter. They sat in my office and explained that they sensed God calling them to pray for me. They made that trip simply to ask for my permission!

It was obvious how seriously they took this call from God. I'm not the only leader they regularly pray for, but I felt encouraged beyond anything words could describe. I still do. When I face tough times as a leader, I know Doug and Sherry are interceding on my behalf. Their prayers have often resulted in words of wisdom for me. That kind of encouragement—spiritual encouragement—is amazing. It keeps me going and inspires me to do the same for others.

Although you must be intentional about being a spiritual encourager, it is not something you add to your to-do list. It's something the Holy Spirit inspires in you as you pray for spiritual discernment and to impact people's lives. The more you ask the Holy Spirit to guide you, the better able you will be to encourage people.

As ministry leaders, we all need encouragement. We all have difficult and discouraging days, but our efforts are not in vain. The work of the kingdom is worth it. You will no doubt get tired, even exhausted, but remember your work matters even when you don't see the results you want. That's the thing about spiritual leadership. You can't see everything happening in the spirit realm, and you won't know all the lives you have impacted for good until you go to heaven. But don't give up. You may not feel you are recognized for all the work you do, but God knows about your efforts. He really does. He gave you your gifts and abilities and delights in your service to Him and His kingdom.

When you need to recharge, take some time to rest. I have learned that it's possible to miss the encouragement that comes your way because you are too tired or discouraged to receive it. Jesus loves it when you laugh and play. Take the time you need to have fun and relax sometimes. When you do, people will enjoy following you!

As a ministry leader, I know you need real people to thank you for the sacrifices you make and the time you spend serving others. So let me be one of them. Thank you for all you do for the kingdom. You matter, and if you have time, I'd love for you to send me a note telling me about your ministry. I really will read it, and I'll take a moment to pray for you and thank God for the work you're doing.

We all need encouragement, but that's just one part of the equation. Leaders who truly want to engage followers must master another skill—inspiration. No leader gets a pass on this. We all must inspire others, or they will not continue to follow us. The good news is that inspiration comes in many different packages.

Chapter Four

INSPIRE PEOPLE TO FOLLOW THE VISION

Inspiring leaders get people to connect with the
vision and open their eyes to new possibilities.

NSPIRATION IS CRITICAL to any leader's success. It is not only one of the ways we draw and keep followers, but it is also how we motivate the people we serve to embrace the vision God has given us. It is how we encourage them to push past their comfort zones and open their hearts to new possibilities. In short, inspiration is a leader's lifeblood.

All effective leaders inspire people. Some may not fit the traditional stereotype of an inspiring leader. They may not be charismatic and have personalities that are larger than life. They may not own the crowd the minute they walk onto a stage. But what truly inspirational leaders have is knowledge. They know *how* they inspire people, and they build on that self-awareness to become more and more inspiring.

It may be hard to believe, but charismatic people with big personalities make up only a small percentage of leaders. Typically, those individuals are operating in a God-given gift that can't be acquired or developed. It's simply an attribute God chose to grant them. Truly inspirational leaders don't need magnanimous personalities to motivate people. They know how to leverage the gifts God has given them and inspire people in the style that best suits them. And you can learn to do the same.

Below are several of the more common means through which leaders inspire people to follow the vision. See if you can identify the one that fits you best.

Relationship

This is a familiar path of inspiration, especially in small and midsize churches. Relational leaders are great shepherds, and their congregations know it. In fact, they feel it. All good leaders love people, but this group of leaders has a special way of expressing that love so it is clearly known. People are lifted to new heights when they know they are loved and cared for. When relationships are solid, committed people will follow and serve faithfully. The downside is that leaders are limited in the number of relationships they can handle. So eventually relational leaders will need to invest their time developing new leaders who return the favor by mentoring another crop of leaders.

Strategy

This group of leaders inspires through their ability to organize, clearly state the next steps, and keep things running smoothly. People dislike chaos, poor communication, and unclear goals with a passion. When a leader shows up who can consistently provide clear direction, the people are moved to follow. Leaders who have a big vision but don't know how to realize it can frustrate those they serve. Strategic inspiration solves that problem, but the downside is that it requires followers to be more mature because it doesn't always feel fun. If you inspire by having great strategy, find ways to make the process enjoyable.

Passion

The leaders in this group are sincere and fired up about the vision. They may lack some leadership skills, but they are true zealots, and people can't help but pursue the vision alongside them. They burn bright, and that draws people to them. The downside is that they may offer unclear direction, and the intensity of their passion can lead to burnout. Strategic inspiration coupled with passionate inspiration is a winning combination, and it would be wise for these two groups of leaders to learn from each other. Those who inspire through passion would be wise to bring a leader alongside them who will complement their style.

Competence

These leaders are so highly skilled and good at what they do that people are inspired to follow them. The leaders in this group are typically more focused in their abilities. In fact, great focus is how they have developed such an expertise, and what they excel in is usually noteworthy. A common example is a pastor who is excellent at expositing Scripture verse by verse. People love a great teacher of the Word, and many will overlook a ministry's weaker areas when the leader has this strength. The downside is that competence will not carry vision over the long haul, so these leaders must take care to nurture relationships at least on a basic level.

Coaching

These leaders are consummate people-developers. They bring out the best in those they lead, and help them become better than they could or would become on their own. Leaders who inspire through coaching are great encouragers. They have a strong ability to know and lean into people's strengths, but they also have a good eye for areas that need improvement. Leaders who are great at coaching are excellent team builders and have an ability to develop strong morale. These leaders get the people to work hard, but they also make sure their followers enjoy the experience and achieve their goals.

> True ministry is not about perfection; it's about continued movement toward the vision.

You may have a blend of two of these styles of inspiration. In rare cases, you might even have traces of a third style. But in general, leaders inspire largely from one of these approaches. If you aren't sure which one fits you best, ask a few leaders who are close to you. I predict they will know the answer without hesitation. It's important that you know your dominant style so you can continue to improve your ability to inspire people to follow the vision.

True ministry is not about perfection; it's about continued movement toward the vision. Inspiration is meant to serve as a positive catalyst for that progress. I have talked about several different ways leaders inspire, and now I'd like to offer you a number of characteristics that mark all leaders who are serious about inspiring the people they serve. These traits will help motivate people to follow your leadership.

INSPIRING LEADERS BRING CHANGE

Churches resist change—some much more than others—and it takes an inspiring leader who is committed to the vision to lead a continual process of change. Ministries that are not changing are slowly dying, and there are no exceptions to this fact. If you have been doing the same things in the same ways for years, it is very likely that your ministry is not as robust as it could be, and in time it will begin to decline.

Change, however, is not arbitrary. As leaders, our intent should never be to make changes merely for the sake of doing something new. At 12Stone Church I often say, "I'm not looking for something different; I'm looking for something better." Change is about improvement and progress, not creating a new brochure. It is essential that your decisions be strategic and intentional as you drive toward the vision.

But if your ministry is anything like most, you will face resistance to change. My friend Gerald Brooks, who is the senior pastor at Grace Outreach Center in Plano, Texas, says, "If you change something and no one gets upset, then you changed something that doesn't matter." That is so true! Earlier I said churches resist change. The truth is that people resist change. In a consultation with a church in Michigan, I recommended that they stop holding Sunday night services. I cited a number of good reasons for this move. Based on their response, you would have thought I'd sworn at them.

The church leaders didn't resist after giving my advice careful consideration. They just rejected the idea outright. The irony is that they brought me in to help them transition to a more streamlined, "simple church" model. They were excited about the idea of moving toward a leaner, more focused ministry model until they bumped into something they didn't want to change!

Jesus began His ministry by calling people to change. He told them to repent of their sins and turn to God (Matt. 4:17). Then He showed them the benefits of change during His Sermon on the Mount (Matt. 5:3-12). Jesus also spent considerable time preparing people for change and challenging them to embrace change when it arrived. (See Luke 5:36-39.) As leaders, a significant portion of our role is to do the same thing. We must inspire people to change and teach them how to adapt to it. This, of course, won't be easy, but you can make the transition smoother by keeping these things in mind:

- Establish the need for change. The people need to know why the change is being made.

- Don't be a lone ranger. Make sure your key leaders are on board with you before you introduce a change to the congregation or your ministry team.

- Make sure the timing is right. Even much-needed changes can be hindered if they are instituted at the wrong time. Take time to plan carefully.

Think about what changes need to be made at the church or ministry where you serve. Consider what, if anything, prevents those changes from being made. Then determine the first or next step you can take toward implementing the necessary change.

INSPIRING LEADERS SEIZE OPPORTUNITIES

Vision is directly connected to opportunity. Kingdom needs are met when leaders see a need God puts before them and act on it. If there is no immediate opportunity, then the visionary leader will search for one. Whether you are a senior pastor, staff member, or volunteer leader, ask God to help you see opportunities.

At 12Stone Church we have some of the most amazing volunteer leaders in our small group ministry. They possess great vision for life change among the people in their groups. I love listening to stories of how they seized opportunities to help people. Recently one small group helped a family that had lost their jobs and their home move into a small apartment the church members helped them find. I've lost count of how often small group members have seized these kinds of opportunities to help people.

> **Leaders who inspire consistently do the right things at the right time so their efforts lead to success.**

Opportunities don't always fall in your lap. In many cases you have to go out and seek them. I introduced you to Norwood Davis earlier, our CFO and director of extension ministries at 12Stone. He is always looking for properties we can use to launch new campuses as part of our multisite church strategy. We have multiple campuses that all broadcast the same sermon, one week delayed, via video. But each site has its own pastor, staff, worship team, small groups, and so on. Much of our ability to reach people for Jesus has come through campus leaders who seized opportunities to meet the needs around them.

Leaders who inspire others ask God to reveal opportunities.

But in all honesty, God reveals many opportunities that leaders miss. You won't see them if you aren't looking. You won't see them if you don't believe God will give them to you. And you won't see them if you are too busy with the daily responsibilities of leadership to pay attention to the things God may be trying to show you. Leaders who inspire consistently do the right things at the right time so their efforts produce success.

INSPIRING LEADERS TAKE RISKS

My friend Joe Centineo took a big risk in 2002. He and his wife, Toni, and their kids put everything on the line and moved from New Jersey to Texas to plant a church. Today Crossroads of Arlington Church is a thriving congregation meeting the needs of hundreds of people. They started meeting in a recreation center, and like most young churches they sacrificed and worked hard setting up and tearing down equipment every Sunday until God gave them a permanent facility.[1] Without that huge risk in 2002, Crossroads would not exist!

Who knows how many people in Joe's congregation or on his leadership team have been inspired to take risks because of their pastor's example. Not every risk is as big at the one Joe took. Some are everyday risks, such as confronting someone in the church about gossip or asking a generous giver for a substantial financial contribution. You may have a difficult presentation to make before the church board. Or perhaps you're the head usher and you must "release" an usher who has been part of the church for years. No matter the situation, all leaders must take risks. It's part of the very nature of leadership.

As I've consulted with pastors and volunteer leaders, I have found three big risk killers that you must pay attention to. First on the list is fear. Every leader who is in touch with reality faces fear. If you are making progress and pressing into uncharted waters, you can't help but to experience some fear. The only way to avoid fear is to sit safely on the sidelines and coast in your leadership. But then you aren't leading. The best antidote for fear is action. Even if it's one small step at a time, take it. A series of little improvements turn into great progress over time.

The second risk killer is perfectionism. The local church was never designed for perfection. People are wonderful, but they are also messy. Projects and programs never go quite as planned, and you'll never have the final answer because life keeps moving. If you wait until everything lines up just right before you take a risk, you will have effectively removed the element of risk. And you also will have probably lost the opportunity. Do your homework, pray, and then take the risk.

The third risk killer is lack of clarity. If you don't know where you are headed, or if the vision is in some way unclear, taking a risk can be foolish. I'm not saying you must be certain about every detail, but you need to be clear about your goal. If you pray to discern God's mind on the issue and seek alignment with your key leaders, then you will be poised to take a prudent risk.

INSPIRING LEADERS DELIVER HOPE

Leaders, like everyone else, don't always know what God will do, but they know His nature. There is a quote attributed to Charles Spurgeon that says it well: "God is too good to be unkind. He is too wise to be confused. If I cannot trace His hand I can always trust His heart."[2]

Obviously, honesty is a nonnegotiable for leaders. But that doesn't mean we can't tap into our own faith in God to inspire people with a message of hope. I'm confident that you firmly believe God loves you and wants the best for you and your church or ministry. This belief allows you to communicate a certain confidence about the future. It doesn't make you a prophet or allow you to make foolish promises. But it makes you a leader who sees a better future and believes God will help people live out that future. At some point your theology will influence how you communicate that hope, but the basics of faith remain true for all leaders who are called according to God's purpose.

Your church may be under pressure. You may be experiencing difficulties, but you know God's heart and can communicate it. For example, many churches are struggling because their income doesn't meet their budget needs. As a leader, you can give hope, no matter what specific function you serve in your organization. You know it is not God's will that your ministry fail. You know it is not God's plan that your evangelism and discipleship programs be rendered ineffective due to a lack of finances. Perhaps the resources are lean because people are not giving according to God's plan. If that is the case, you can inspire them to trust God with their finances by sharing a positive, hope-filled message.

Perhaps you find it difficult to deliver hope because you are discouraged yourself. I do not take that lightly. Leadership can be lonely and difficult at times. But at some point, you must dig deep into your own faith in God, remind yourself of His promises to you, and communicate that to the people you serve. I'm not suggesting you "fake it till you make it." I never recommend that. In fact, you may need to spend some quality time with friends and colleagues who can help restore your faith. But ultimately it is your responsibility as a leader to trust God and have confidence in His Word so you can communicate hope to the people, whether on a small or large scale. The hope you deliver is a crucial element to inspire people to follow your leadership.

INSPIRING LEADERS DEMONSTRATE DISCIPLINE

Discipline is rarely listed among the attributes that make a leader inspiring. The truth is, however, a leader who lacks discipline is wholly and completely uninspiring. I'm confident you can name more than one talented leader, perhaps a leader more gifted than you are, who can never seem to get his act together. The kingdom loses when this happens, and so do those leaders. The undisciplined leader, though potentially high-performing, is often unprepared. This leader tends to do things at the last minute and is prone to change his mind to try the latest cool trend or hot new idea. That is not motivating to anyone.

This may surprise you, but people would much rather follow someone who may not be amazingly talented but is reliable. It's because they can trust them. A disciplined lifestyle is difficult to maintain. Everyone knows that. So when people see a leader who demonstrates discipline, they are inspired. They begin to believe they can live out a similar discipline. When I talk about discipline, I'm not referring to a strange, over-the-top, ascetic kind of lifestyle. But I want to refrain from listing specific markers of a disciplined life. That can get pharisaic fast. Yet we all know that being disciplined in areas such as physical health, emotional integrity, spiritual vitality, and intellectual development will pay huge dividends in the long run.

I advise you to tackle one area at a time. This is so you don't impose a legalistic set of rules upon yourself that you end up discarding in a short time. Pick one or two areas and dig in. Set some personal goals. And make it fun.

I've been jogging for years. I typically run about twenty-five miles a week, but recently I managed to injure my right foot. Too many miles for too many years. My podiatrist wouldn't let me run for months. He allowed me to ride only a stationary bike. Rather than calling him the devil, I decided to make bicycling fun until I could run again. Although I still prefer jogging, my real priority was to not let anything prevent me from continuing the discipline of exercise. (I had to smile when I discovered the doctor attends 12Stone. And I'm happy to report my foot is nearly as good as new. Thanks, Doc!)

Living a disciplined life doesn't mean you put yourself in bondage. Identify one area you should work on and start there. And think long-term. Don't set unrealistic goals, which can lead to discouragement, burnout, or both. Start small. Do something you can imagine continuing for a lifetime. The results will be worth it, I promise.

Inspiring Leaders Express a Consistent Level of Confidence

Let me ask you a leading question. What is the source of your confidence? Don't be too quick to answer. You may want to say God is your source, but if your confidence often wavers, swinging up and down, then it is in something other than God. I know that's true for me. When I lean on my own abilities to make something happen, my confidence often falters. I have a steady sense of confidence only when I embrace the reality that God's Spirit lives in me doing what I cannot do.

This is a tricky line for spiritual leaders to walk. The distance between humility and arrogance is short. Extreme or false humility does not inspire, and arrogance repels people. Yet receiving God's gifts and favor is such an incredibly humbling experience, it allows you to operate with a "God confidence" that doesn't waver.

This humble, or quiet, confidence that comes from God is the foundation of your strength as a leader. But there are two other factors that are intricately connected to consistent confidence. First is having a healthy self-image. Seeing yourself as God made you—nothing more and nothing less—is a great place to start. From there it's important to surround yourself with a small circle of people who love and care about you and will tell you the truth.

Second, you must begin to put some successes under your belt. Don't worry if the successes are small. Gaining personal momentum is more important than taking down the big win. Your small successes will gradually turn into larger ones.

Below are a series of questions you can ask yourself to assess your confidence level as a leader. If you identify areas that are lacking, focus on improving them. I guarantee it will be worth the effort.

Assessing Your Confidence Internally	Assessing Your Confidence Externally
Are you utterly dependent upon God?	Are you good at what you do? How do you know?
Do you intentionally resist your most powerful temptation?	Do your peers recognize you as a competent leader?
Are there any sin issues you are not honest about?	Do you consistently prepare to the best of your ability?
Do you understand your security and significance in Christ?	Are you a student of leadership? What are you learning? How are you improving?

Is your home life in order?	How do you transfer knowledge into applied wisdom?
Do you see yourself as a disciplined person?	What is your leadership Achilles' heel, and how do you protect yourself from this weakness?
How are you cultivating the fruit of the Spirit in your life?	When it comes to tangible leadership successes, what is your "batting average"?

INSPIRING LEADERS COMMUNICATE VISION IN A COMPELLING WAY

When Bill Hybels spoke at 12Stone (then called Crossroads Church) in 2002, he delivered an incredibly inspiring talk on reaching people who are not followers of Christ. He was transparent with us as he spoke of an experience that softened his heart toward the lost. He said every day when he arrived home, he'd toss the junk mail in the trash before he went from the garage into his house. One night he tossed a postcard with pictures of missing children on the front. As the missing persons flyer fluttered down into the trash can, Bill said it struck him as strange that he didn't seem to care.

God spoke to him in that moment and asked, "What if they were your kids?" Bill knew that if the children were his own, he'd do anything to find them. Then God said, "They are *My* kids!" That experience changed the way he viewed the lost, and it has impacted Willow Creek Community Church in a huge way. My brief summary barely does the story justice. But I assure you, the people in the service that day received a clear and compelling picture of Bill's vision to reach the lost. And many were inspired to do more to engage with those who don't know Christ.

Not every leader is a great communicator or vision-caster. In fact, many leaders are vision-carriers. That means a leader above them has set and cast the vision and expects them to carry it to others. Both vision-casters and vision-carriers are essential for a ministry to thrive, especially a local church. Whatever your leadership role, the practices listed below will go a long way toward helping you communicate vision more effectively.

- Commit to the vision yourself. As the leader, no one cares more about fulfilling the vision than you do. No one carries a greater burden or lies awake at night thinking and praying more than you do. Your passion and commitment for the vision must be profound.

- Capture the hearts of the people. You do this by first giving the people your heart. Your honesty, authenticity, and vulnerability help people connect with you and feel the message you want them to respond to.

- Clearly identify the current situation. Whatever the current reality is, make sure the people understand it. Whether you are the senior pastor, choir director, or lead the children's ministry team, start by presenting the facts.

- Paint a picture of a preferred future. After you have given a clear picture of the present, describe the better future you envision. Explain why it's better and how they will benefit.

- Deliver clear direction with a realistic plan. Let the people know exactly where you are headed and why. And show them a written plan explaining how you will get there. The plan should be simple but well thought out.

- Tell the people they are needed and show them how to participate. When the people hear the plan, they should see themselves as part of bringing it to pass. They should easily see how they fit in.

- Keep the lines of communication open. Casting the vision is just the beginning. Keep the people well informed of the progress. Share both setbacks and successes.

- Celebrate the victories! Thank God for what He is doing and enjoy the journey.

Inspiring people to connect to the vision is at the core of a ministry's mission and future success. But I hope you can see by now that being an inspiring leader isn't about having a big personality. It's about consistently doing the right things at the right time. Thankfully, the art, skill, and passion needed to inspire others can be improved over the course of a lifetime. And the persistence to develop these skills is what will produce success.

AMPLIFY YOUR LEADERSHIP

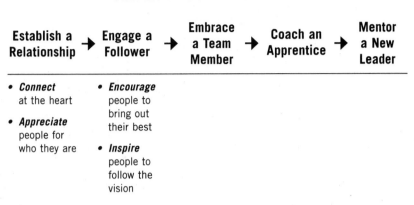

Establish a Relationship →	Engage a Follower →	Embrace a Team Member →	Coach an Apprentice →	Mentor a New Leader
• *Connect* at the heart	• *Encourage* people to bring out their best			
• *Appreciate* people for who they are	• *Inspire* people to follow the vision			

As you can see, this process of expanding your leadership builds layer upon layer. It is important that you keep the big picture in mind because it takes time to grasp the overall process and a lifetime of practicing it to reap its full benefit. After you have established a relationship and engaged a follower, it's time to embrace a team member. This third part of the process requires two skills that often separate great leaders from average ones—the ability to *invite* and the commitment to *equip.*

PART
THREE

EMBRACE A TEAM MEMBER

A great team is what makes the tapestry of leadership beautiful.

O F THE NUMEROUS books I've read on the subject of teamwork, Patrick Lencioni's *The Five Dysfunctions of a Team* is
easily in the top three. Using a creative fable about a high-
tech start-up company, Lencioni describes a five-step process that
will turn dysfunction into performance. I highly recommend the
book and won't attempt to improve on his work here. Instead, I
want to briefly hone in on what he identifies as the foundation of
any successful team: trust.

There are, of course, many types of trust. One type of trust is
the confidence we have in our team members to do what they say
they will do. This is a very important type of trust, but it's not the

only one that forms the foundation of a good team. Every productive team needs the kind of trust that allows them to be real with one another and to share their hearts without fear of condemnation or repercussion.

As the executive pastor at 12Stone Church, I have the privilege of leading our incredible team of staff, a group that models the kind of trust Lencioni writes about. I can't speak highly enough of the group I serve with, and it's not because things always run smoothly and no one ever makes mistakes. Every day brings a wonderful combination of significant challenge and pure joy. This truly is a great combination. If there were no challenges, that would mean we weren't making progress. And without joy, the never-ending process of handling difficulties would be intolerable.

Our overall ministry team is made up of both paid staff and volunteer leaders. They are all highly gifted and motivated people, but as we discuss teamwork, I will focus on the paid staff. Our team is large, and it's more like a combination of a posse and a rock band than a conventional staff. They ride hard, shoot fast, and make some killer music along the way.

There is no pretense with this group. What you see is what you get. It's a casual bunch. No coats and ties (though there's nothing wrong with suits; I wore them for twenty years), and you might even see flip-flops on occasion. But they are serious about their calling and what they do. They often say, "We don't take ourselves too seriously, but we take God very seriously." This is really true about us.

During our monthly staff meeting, after our senior pastor, Kevin Myers, teaches a great leadership lesson, we have a tradition of presenting two awards. We call them the Good Bird and the Dirty Bird awards. The awards are funky, wildly decorated ceramic birds, and their history is as colorful as the statues themselves, but

I won't go into that just now. The Good Bird is awarded to the staff member who most exemplified amazing servant leadership that month. The Dirty Bird is a completely different story. This is our equivalent of the Dumb and Dumber Award, and it's given to the person who did something *really dumb* that month.

Now before you start thinking we're heartless and cruel, let me assure you that the staff enjoys winning the Dirty Bird more than the Good Bird. I'm proud to say I have won it many times myself. We don't celebrate mistakes, but we want the team to know they are valued despite their missteps, and it is important that we laugh at ourselves. We still trust them as leaders. Our team is on a journey together to accomplish God's vision for our church and community. No one is a lone ranger.

Thanks to the leadership of Kevin Myers, there is little to no politics on the team. This is a great gift and, frankly, a huge asset. Staff politics that include petty jealousies, power plays, gossip, dishonesty, and a lack of loving confrontation will kill any team. Through the grace of God and intentional effort on our parts, we are able to keep politics almost entirely out of our mix.

As Lencioni notes in his book (which you really should read if you have the time), the ability to handle conflict constructively helps build commitment on the team. We see that at 12Stone, which I refer to merely as a point of reference. You can use our team to make a healthy comparison in order to learn and grow from our successes and mistakes. I'm sure some things about our staff are making you feel really good about your team, but there may be other elements that inspire you and your team to pursue new heights.

The 12Stone team works hard. I would be the last person to question their commitment. They are motivated and truly care about what they do. We don't have to worry about how many hours the staff keeps. In fact, it is more likely that we have to make sure they are taking their days off and getting the time they need to stay fresh and energized.

Pastor Chris Huff, a former engineer and atheist who is now one of our top leaders (we're pretty sure he's saved), recently officiated at three funerals in twenty-four hours. That was an incredible effort. He had to prepare three sermons, make arrangements for the services, and care for the families. On top of that he was leading the parking lot team at the Central campus and working on the technology to launch our Internet campus while juggling about a dozen other things! Great team members carry their share and then some.

The staff is undeniably talented, but I truly believe it is their commitment to the church's vision that makes them such a high-capacity bunch. Diane Heller is the executive assistant to Kevin Myers. Anyone who's met her knows she's the one who really runs the church. We're all afraid of Diane—well, not really, but we probably should be. When you walk into her office, you are guaranteed two things—a warm smile and chocolate from the little dish on her desk. After that, who knows what will happen.

Diane can juggle more tasks than anyone I know, and she does it all well. She identifies needs in the church and is right much more often than I care to admit. Kevin receives dozens and dozens of requests for appointments and help meeting various needs. He couldn't possibly respond to each one. His schedule is extremely demanding, and the staff is more than capable of handling what he can't get to. Diane takes care of all those requests and much more, and she makes people feel good about seeing someone other than the senior pastor. When a church or ministry has a talented team, it experiences greater effectiveness and can be resilient even in difficult times.

As you may have guessed, I have the utmost respect for our team, and we genuinely like each other. Pastor Shannon Whaples is dedicated to prayer, and I never tire of hearing him go to God with the needs of our team members and the church. Shannon loves Jesus, and it comes through when he prays and in how he lives. Of all the great leadership qualities I've seen in Shannon, his commitment to Jesus is the first thing that comes to my mind. How cool is that!

It's important that you like the people you are with forty to fifty hours a week. When I was younger, I hired for competence first. Now I hire for chemistry. Of course, competence matters, but typically there are many applicants who can do the job. The real questions are, Will we want to work together, and will we work together well? If that chemistry doesn't exist, it won't matter how competent the individuals are or how amazing their résumés look. If you wouldn't want to hang out with the people you work with on your day off, you may be missing an important element of chemistry on your team.

Pastor Mark Eiken is one of those guys who helps create great chemistry. He is our resident Lutheran and Minnesota Vikings lover, and even though he doesn't like the Beatles (an illness I can't figure out or solve for him), I let him remain on staff. I'm kidding, of course. We are blessed to have Mark on staff. He is a highly gifted leader who inspires others and makes things happen. I can't imagine our 12Stone team without him.

I recently traveled to North Carolina to invest a day teaching leadership to a group of pastors. Three of our sharp young pastors came with me. The evening before the conference the four of us jumped into my car, and we took off for Kings Mountain, North Carolina. We had a great time together talking about everything from marriage to some of the ideas in this book. Those guys drink more Starbucks than anyone I've ever met, and I now know enough about Southern barbecue to last me for a lifetime. But I wouldn't trade my time with them for anything!

I trust our 12Stone team with my whole heart. The integrity runs deep. And that's what forms the foundation of our team. It's not about perfection. We're nowhere close to perfect, but the people here are the real deal and their character is reliable. I can count on them to be who they say they are and do what they say they will do. It's difficult to communicate how much it means to work with a group like that—people who will admit to a mistake they made and take responsibility to clean it up. Having that kind of trust in the people I work with is priceless.

I love the 12Stone staff. They are unquestionably some of the most extraordinary people I know. But building a great team does not happen by chance. In the next two chapters we'll look closely at two essential skills for developing a winning team, beginning with the ability to effectively *invite* people to join you in ministry.

Chapter Five

INVITE INDIVIDUALS INTO
MEANINGFUL MINISTRY

An invitation to engage in meaningful ministry
is an opportunity to change lives.

THERE ARE TWO kinds of invitations. One invites you to an
event you'd like to attend and the other to something you'd
rather avoid. As leaders, we must learn how to skillfully extend
invitations of the first kind.

Not long ago Patti and I were invited to attend James Taylor
and Carole King's Live at the Troubadour concert at the Gwinnett
Arena in Atlanta. We had tried to get tickets, but the concert sold
out in an hour. So it's an understatement to say we were thrilled

when Chris Morgan, 12Stone's incredibly gifted worship leader, and his wife, Mary Anne, invited us to attend the concert with them. We said yes in a heartbeat. And we weren't disappointed. The concert was one of the best we've ever attended.

In great contrast, I once received an invitation from a local church to serve as their executive pastor. I won't tell you about the church. There is no need to be unkind, but suffice it to say that accepting the invitation would have been the door to my worst nightmare—and perhaps theirs too. I couldn't decline fast enough.

We all know the difference between invitations that draw us in and those that drive us away. When we're on the giving end of an invitation, we want the person to accept it. But we know any invitation can be declined. After all, an invitation is basically a question, and it will provoke a yes or no response. There's simply no way around that.

As ministry leaders, we want our invitations to be hard to resist. But no matter how badly we may want someone to join our team, our invitations must never resemble a high-pressure sales tactic. Whether the person is being invited to serve as staff or in a volunteer position, he should never feel as though his arm is being twisted. It's only right that he have the opportunity to think and pray about the decision and ultimately to follow the Lord's leading. But we pray they say yes, as my friend Jason Britt did.

In the fall of 2010, 12Stone launched a Saturday service at our Central campus. Jason, the campus pastor, had about eight weeks to recruit and build the ministry teams before the first Saturday service. Jason and his team prayed about their need for the new campus and cast vision for the venture. Then they invited a couple hundred people to jump in and serve—and they did! The people connected with the vision and signed on!

Jesus was a master at extending invitations that were hard to refuse. Yes, He was the Son of God, but people said no to Jesus too. One of Jesus's most famous invitations is found in Matthew 4:19. He told Andrew and Peter, "Come, follow Me...and I will make you fishers of men." I don't think Jesus said that casually or as if Peter's and Andrew's responses didn't matter to Him. Jesus *wanted* them to follow Him. He knew their purpose was rolled up in their answer to that invitation. The stakes were incredibly high.

As ministry leaders, we're not inviting people to a movie. We're inviting them to join a team of people committed to leading meaningful ministry. We're inviting them to become part of a cause, a vision, something big that changes people's lives. We are inviting them to partner with us in advancing the kingdom. The stakes are very high.

Responding to your invitation may connect someone with the ministry God is calling her to. Or it may put her in a position to make a life-altering impact on someone in the church or community. We don't always know what God will do with someone's yes, but we know this: it matters whether that person joins your team. This is why it's so important for leaders to know how to extend a compelling invitation.

TAKE PERSONAL INVENTORY

Leaders who receive great responses to their appeals understand that extending a compelling invitation is a skill, and they are willing to do the hard work to develop it. And trust me, it can be hard work because often the thing keeping us from drawing people to our team lies within. If people perceive you as hard to please or lacking confidence, they won't be drawn to join your team. So if you're serious about building a great ministry team, you'll need to deal with your own stuff first. I've listed several questions below that will help you take personal inventory and, perhaps, identify characteristics that may be driving people away from you.

Are you honest about your goals?

The word *recruit* is often used to describe the process of bringing new people onto a team. It's a strong word that includes the idea of getting the job done. To be blunt, it means getting a yes or closing the deal. Recruit is a good word, but to be perfectly candid, I struggled over which term is better, invite or recruit. I have concluded that invite is a better term because it communicates our true intent. And it represents well the relational nature of leadership in ministry. But anyone who has ever been tasked with finding volunteers to serve on a team knows the invitation contains elements very similar to recruiting.

My former neighbor was a recruiter for the Atlanta Falcons. His job was to spot talent and get that person on the team. He didn't have a cup of coffee with a three hundred-pound lineman, "invite" him to join the Falcons, and cross his fingers hoping the guy would say yes. His job was to close the deal.

In the church, our goal is to accomplish a kingdom cause and develop lasting relationships. But leaders do close deals, or we'd get nothing done. Being honest with yourself about that fact is a healthy place to start developing your ability to draw new leaders and volunteers.

Are you a control freak?

Most leaders have a little control freak in them. When I was younger, I had a lot of control freak in me. At one point in my life, I had appointed myself general manager of the universe. It took a while, but God finally convinced me that He could keep Planet

Earth spinning without me. In fact, I started to repeat the mantra "God is in control." But I soon learned this wasn't enough. I had to say, "God is in control, and I'm not." It's funny how we can't see what we can't see. People do not respond well to control freaks. They never have, and they never will. People want to be part of a team that values what they bring to the table and allows them to make a contribution.

Are you a perfectionist?

Get over thinking that no one can do it as well as you can. Sure, there are plenty of people who don't have your skill set, but there are others who will run rings around you if given the chance. Perfectionism will cast a negative shadow over any invitation. Having high standards and a spirit of excellence are good, but perfectionism is a waste of time. People are not drawn to tasks they can never accomplish. They will consistently turn down invitations from leaders they can never please. If the people you're inviting don't know you are a perfectionist, they may say yes and join the ministry team. But as soon as they discover your perfectionism, they will quit. I'm not suggesting you lower your standards, but strive for progress not perfection.

Do you procrastinate?

Leaders procrastinate for a variety of reasons that are sometimes difficult to discern. The root issue could be a lack of discipline, misaligned priorities, or good old-fashioned fear. Whatever the underlying cause, people can sense when a leader's timing is off. They may not be able to put their finger on the root problem, but they know when something is amiss, and they will not be drawn to that leader. When people sense that a leader is procrastinating, they will likely pass on that person's invitations. Most people are busy, and they want to be part of things that are progressive and productive, not projects being stalled by procrastination.

Are you fearful of being turned down?

No one likes rejection. But as leaders, we have to remember that when someone says no, it's usually not personal. In fact, the reason for that response is almost always tied to the person who declined the invitation. And the reason isn't necessarily negative. The person might simply be engaged in ministry already.

Fear of rejection is intricately connected to insecurity. If you struggle with this type of fear, I strongly suggest you address it by building the kind of God confidence I spoke of in chapter 4. If you don't, insecurity will consistently prevent you from extending compelling invitations. People connect with causes or ministries they believe in, but they are also drawn to confident leaders. To communicate your confidence when you extend invitations, focus on the importance of the ministry and your concern for the people receiving it.

Do you fail to see the potential in people?

If you don't acknowledge the potential you see in the people being invited to join a ministry team, they will think you just want to fill a slot. All church leaders have faced the pressure to meet a personnel need, whether that position is volunteer or full-time. The tension to have enough workers for the ministry to function at maximum capacity will never go away. It's how you handle that tension that makes the difference.

Don't make your pressure their problem. Absorb it. Stay focused on the ministry's mission and value the person joining the team. If you don't honestly believe the ministry opportunity will positively impact the individual, don't extend the invitation. But for most people, serving in ministry is an opportunity to grow spiritually and develop untapped gifts. When a leader can see this kind of potential in people and communicate it to them, rarely will their invitation be turned down.

CONNECT WITH A PERSON'S PASSION

Reciprocity is more than negotiating a win-win scenario. It's developing a mutually beneficial relationship, one that maintains a healthy balance of give and take, and respect. No one likes to be taken advantage of, and no one likes to feel patronized.

One of the great challenges for ministry leaders is to remember that the people God gives us to lead are not there just to get a job done. I know that for busy leaders, this is a difficult tension to negotiate. In any growing church, there is always work to be done, and leaders face pressure to find people to do it. But when you're inviting people into meaningful ministry, it's critical that you don't make them feel like cogs in a wheel. You must connect with their passion, gifts, and desires—especially if you want your team members to stick around for any length of time. My daughter, Mackenzie, is an aspiring young filmmaker. She has talent, passion, and big dreams to pursue a career within the motion picture industry. When the leaders at 12Stone discovered her passion, she was quickly recruited from children's ministry to the video and film teams. She has been enthusiastically involved for many years now. This is, of course, the ideal scenario, but sometimes we just need someone to say yes.

There are two questions to keep in mind in order manage to this tension between meeting your need for volunteers and connecting people with their passion.

What does the mission require?

As a leader, you have to make things happen. You need to move the ball down the field. If you don't make progress, you're just spinning your wheels. In certain areas of ministry, it is nonnegotiable to find qualified volunteers. Take children's ministry for instance. Any church leader will want a world-class children's ministry because it is a key draw for young families. But to be done well, children's ministry requires a huge number of volunteer leaders and ministry teams. That's a lot of pressure for a leader, and it comes every week. You can't have seventeen babies in the nursery and no adult to care for them.

Jenny Luongo, the nursery ministry team leader at 12Stone's Central campus, faces this dilemma every week. Every Sunday about one hundred fifty babies fill the church's nursery (that would scare me to death!), so Jenny has no choice but to constantly invite people to join her team. She's not recruiting them to a task but to a vision. She loves the kids and believes she and her team can impact those children and their parents. Instead of communicating the church's need for more workers, Jenny shares the significance of the mission. In this way she presents a powerful invitation!

What does the person desire?

As a leader, you must always balance numbers. You'll need a certain number of people to make things happen in your ministry, but you can't see people as numbers. A great test is to ask yourself if you are interested in the team members' fulfillment and growth more than getting the job done. People want to feel needed, valued, and cared for. They want to make a difference. The people in your church or ministry will accept your invitation because it gives them opportunity to make a significant contribution. It allows them to support a cause that matters to them.

At 12Stone Church we have teams of people who serve free coffee. They set up, serve, and clean up for thousands of people. That's not a glamorous ministry, but those individuals accepted the invitation because they see the bigger picture, and they know that what they do matters. They also know that we care about them and appreciate what they do. When you as a leader connect the needs of the mission with an individual's desire to make a dif-

> **You will get out of an invitation what you put into it.**

ference, you will strike a much-needed balance and have a winning combination.

MAKE AN INVESTMENT

You will get out of an invitation what you put into it. It's something I call the principle of investment and return. In the context of ministry, leaders primarily make two kinds of investments. First is their investment into building the ministry itself. And second is their investment into the people who join ministry teams. This is where leaders communicate their heart toward the people serving in ministry. And sometimes the message sent isn't the one intended.

Here's a real-world example. Let's say one of the leaders sees Bob while walking down a hall in the church and calls out to him, "Hey, Bob, wanna be an usher?" Instead of communicating that Bob would make a great usher, the leader basically let Bob know he needed a warm body to meet a need. This is definitely *not* an attractive invitation. If, however, the leader sat down with Bob over a cup of coffee, heard his story, and cast vision for the ushers team, the difference would be staggering. The leader would be communicating that he cares about who Bob is as a person. And Bob would be more likely to accept his invitation to become an usher. The leader's results would equal his investment.

The bigger the "ask," the greater the investment required. I am often tasked with hiring new staff. When I invite someone to join our team at 12Stone, I'm usually making a big ask. Often, the person must move from his hometown, friends, and family. Because I'm asking the individual to make such a big decision, I generally spend a significant amount of time with him. I want that person to know we value what he brings to the table and believe his passion and goals line up with our church's mission. When done right, the invitation communicates the huge rewards for both the potential staff member and 12Stone.

There are times when you will need to print an announcement for volunteers in the church bulletin, post a notice online, or address the congregation from the platform. All these tactics are helpful, but the best invitations are made in person, face-to-face. If the invitation matters, make it personal. I've received many invitations by mail, but the ones that also included a phone call or some kind of personal contact made a much greater impact. You may be thinking this whole idea of inviting someone is really time-consuming. It is, and you get out of it what you put in!

SET THE TABLE WELL

A leader's ability to gather people to meetings and special events is intricately connected to his knack for drawing people to join her team. Here's a simple picture. Two people throw a party. One is so packed you can barely move. The other has three people who end up eating up a lot of guacamole by themselves. What made one party such a boom and the other a bust? One person did a better job of setting the table well.

No, I'm not talking about the chips and guacamole. I have met so many pastors who say they invite their people to training meetings and similar events, but the people don't show. The pastors, understandably frustrated, go on and on about the congregation's lack of commitment. I tell those leaders that commitment may be a factor, but it's more likely that they were out-gathered. All the people they wanted at their training meeting were somewhere else—they were at a table that was set better.

I know as ministers we're competing with a culture that gives people hundreds of options. But every day we all choose activities that present the greatest value to us. If the local theater does a better job of attracting people (setting the table), don't get upset with the moviegoers. Do a better job of setting the table. That means you need to provide something people see value in and want to be part of. I promise you, people will beat a path to anything they think is worthwhile.

Patti and I used to attend North Point Community Church before we accepted the invitation from 12Stone to join the team. Andy Stanley is an incredible communicator, and one of the proofs is in North Point's parking lot. You have to love North Point to negotiate the congested parking lot, and people do—by the thousands. People navigate the packed parking lot because Andy Stanley and the team set the table so well they don't want to miss a Sunday!

Don't get me wrong, North Point does a great job handling the traffic. The church is prepared for the crowd. It's just that the traffic is serious. Any ministry that truly wants to set a good table must be ready before the people show up. When you are well prepared for a meeting—whether with one person or one hundred people—you communicate that you value the people attending. If you are running around doing last-minute things and appear unprepared, you communicate the opposite. Even if in your heart you do value the attendees' time, they won't *feel* that way if you are not organized. And you'll hurt your ability to gather them again.

The good news is that people in the local church do give second chances, but they won't do that forever. In a short time they will want to see that there was a good reason for them to show up—even if it was just because they had fun and enjoyed your company! Set the table in such a way that people perceive personal benefit because they took the time to show up.

Being an effective gatherer is not driven by personality but intentionality. You have to bring energy to the mix, but you don't have to be the person in the room with the big, magnetic personality. In fact, while leaders like that are fun and people like them, that kind of charisma can actually distract people from the real purpose. You don't want people to show up because of who will be there. You want them to connect with the real purpose for the gathering.

Intentionality requires clear communication, a thoughtful strategy, and a compelling vision for the purpose of the meeting. Leaders who are good gatherers love life and people. They laugh easily, possess a natural curiosity, and have a positive outlook. People want to be around good gatherers, and they are apt to say yes to their invitations!

Avoid the Classic Mistakes

In my years of mentoring leaders, I've seen pastors make many mistakes as they seek to build their teams. I've made more than a few myself. To help prevent you from repeating those missteps, I want to explore several of the more common mistakes leaders make when extending invitations.

Applying too much pressure

This is not the same as being under pressure. If you are leading, you will always deal with pressure. Acknowledge the reality of the pressure you're facing, but don't transfer it to the person or persons you are asking to join your team. Desperation is a major turnoff, and it will kill an otherwise good invitation. When I talk with college students who want to find the love of their life and get married, I always tell them to relax and let nature take its course. Desperation won't work. If a person tries to get someone to like him because he feels pressure to get married, the relationship stands little chance of working out. But if he asks the right person at the right time, keeping that individual's interests in mind, the results will be dramatically different.

Always inviting the "home team"

I have touched on this briefly, but this is so important I want to reiterate it. Inviting the same people each time there's a need is not expedient; it's lazy. It will hurt your leadership and your church in the long run. Always inviting the home team indicates two problems. First, it shows you are spending too much time with people who are already committed to the ministry and therefore are not establishing new relationships. Second, it means you are wearing out the faithful ones, many of whom are already doing too much.

If you are leading a small church and have a limited number of people to work with, there are two things you can do. First, reduce the number of ministries you offer in your church. And second, invest more time in the people who are attending but not yet serving.

Promoting someone out of his sweet spot

I've done this more times than I care to admit. The situation played out like this. Someone was doing a great job in a ministry area. Then a need arose in another area. So I moved the person. I always thought, "Well, it's a promotion. That's a good thing." But that's not always the case. All too often the person is promoted beyond his level of competence or outside the area of his passion—or both—just to get a job done. If you believe you must move someone out of his sweet spot to fill an urgent need, commit to return that person to a more appropriate position within a short period of time.

Extending an invitation without preparation

If your goal is to invite people to join your team, it's important that you're ready for them. Too often, leaders will extend invitations without being adequately prepared for a response. They haven't set clear expectations, developed a training process, or created opportunities for the new people to get to know the rest of the team. I've consulted with several churches that conducted "ministry fairs." The purpose of the fair was to showcase several ministries and invite people to join the team of their choice. Dozens of people would sign up, but the team leaders would have to say, "We're sorry, but we don't have any more open spots." That was a huge leadership mistake. The people were inspired, took a step forward to serve, and were turned away! You can guess what those individuals will do the next time an invitation comes their way.

Inviting and abandoning

No one likes to be abandoned, especially someone who volunteers his time. I've listened to many highly capable people tell me they quit their ministry team because they basically never heard from their leader again after they were "recruited." That may sound like an exaggeration, but it's pretty close to the truth. The volunteers may have received an occasional e-mail with a new schedule or a thank-you in the hall, but that's about it.

Your team needs to know they are appreciated. They need to be shepherded and nurtured. They need consistent communication, and training is critical. In fact, equipping is so important I'm devoting the next chapter to the subject.

THE COMPONENTS OF A COMPELLING INVITATION

Now that you know what not to do, we'll explore the elements that make invitations irresistible. Before anything else happens, your appeal must be bathed in prayer. No matter how urgent your ministry need, you want the Holy Spirit to handpick the people who will serve on your team. Some of those individuals will need the Lord to prick their hearts about serving. Others may ultimately be led toward a different area of ministry than they expected.

At the other end of your invitation is more than a yes or no. On the other end are all the lives those new team members will touch. On the other end is the building of Christ's kingdom and the realization of His vision for the church or ministry you lead. The importance of prayer cannot be overstated.

After you have committed your invitation to prayer, following the process below will help ensure your invitation hits the intended target and gets a good hearing.

1. Make sure your focus is on maturing believers, not filling slots.

Your goal as a leader is to help people mature spiritually, relationally, and professionally. That should be the motivation behind your invitation—even before fulfilling the vision of the ministry.

If your reason for inviting someone to serve on your team is to give him an opportunity to grow, then that person ultimately will help the ministry progress. It doesn't work the other way around. Effective ministries build people not programs.

Jesus modeled a serving lifestyle. Mark 10:45 says, "For even the Son of Man did not come to be served, but to serve, and to give his life as a ransom for many." Serving is essential to a believer's maturity. Although the serving heart of Jesus is set within us at the point of conversion, we are not immediately motivated by a sacrificial love for others. Serving changes this and helps us develop into mature followers of Jesus.

> **When you invite people to join your team, connect them to a vision not a task.**

2. Share the vision not the task.

When you invite someone to join your team, connect them to a vision for changing lives, not to a specific task. For example, if you invite members to serve on the children's ministry team, tell them how they can impact a child's life. Don't tell them they're needed for storytelling time or to lead a small group. The specific ministry need is important, but in the face of mundane tasks, it's easy to lose sight of the bigger picture. People may lose enthusiasm and even quit if they don't know how they support the larger vision of the ministry.

When Pastor Chris Huff and Jimmy Lastinger, two great leaders at 12Stone, invite people to join the parking team, they cast vision. They make it clear that the ministry is about getting people into the worship auditorium to hear the Word of God with as little stress and hassle as possible. It's not just about directing traffic and parking cars. Our parking team loves their ministry because they know they are changing lives. This is also why they do an incredible job even when it's freezing cold, pouring rain, or hot enough to fry an egg on the hood of a car (not that I've tried that).

3. Communicate the expectations clearly and candidly.

After communicating the vision, talk about the actual responsibilities of the ministry position. It's best to have it in writing so that expectations are clear. Again, in the example of the parking team, each new person must know where he is stationed in the lot, whom he reports to, what time he is on duty, and exactly what he is to do. If those expectations aren't clear, cars would be backed up for miles, and we'd hit gridlock in a matter of minutes on any given Sunday. The volunteers will need training in the specific responsibilities of the position, so leaders, make sure you are prepared.

4. Make the ask.

You would be surprised at how many well-intentioned leaders make compelling spiels about their ministry's vision and needs but never actually ask people to serve. If you allow the "invitation" language to get fuzzy, the person will be left to consider the invite but not to act on it. If there is no question on the table, there is no compelling reason to answer. When I receive an invitation to an event and it requests an RSVP, I always feel responsible to respond. In contrast, without an RSVP, I don't feel a need to answer. There is no real request, nothing compelling me to acknowledge my intent to accept or decline the offer. When you extend an invitation, make sure you also solicit a response. Be personal. Don't just let the individuals know how much you would love to have them on your team. Also go the next step and tell them you would be thrilled should God direct them to accept. Leaders want people to say yes.

It's OK for you to be pleased that God has used you to add someone to the team.

5. Follow up in a timely manner.

If you present an invitation to join a ministry and the person you invited doesn't reply within three days, it's appropriate for you to give him a call. Offer to answer any questions and let the person know you are praying for him. It's OK to ask if the person has made a decision. Most people will know that's why you are calling. The more personal you can be, the better. But if you are working with a large number of invitations, you may need to use e-mail or a social media format such as Facebook. Another option is to organize the callback list into groups of twenty to twenty-five people, and assign a staff member or volunteer leader to follow up with each group so the interaction can be personal.

Extending a compelling invitation is one of the most important parts of your job as a leader. But after your team is in place, they must be equipped to do the work.

Chapter Six

EQUIP YOUR TEAM FOR MINISTRY SUCCESS

Good training sets team members up for ministry success.

JESUS MODELED THE principle of equipping as He trained the disciples. Mark 9:14–29 tells the story of a boy who was possessed by an evil spirit. The boy's dad asked the disciples to drive out the demon, but they couldn't do it. So the man brought his son to Jesus, who of course cast the evil spirit out. The disciples were confused by what happened and asked Jesus why they couldn't drive the evil spirit away. Jesus told them, "This kind can come out by nothing but prayer and fasting" (NKJV).

This is the essence of equipping—not only teaching someone how to engage in ministry but also actually showing him what to do. Jesus wasn't OK with the disciples not casting out the demon. This is why He completed the process for them. Success in our ministry efforts matters to Jesus. When we are equipped and empowered by the Spirit of God, our ministry should be effective.

At one point in the story of the demonized boy, Jesus became frustrated with the boy's father and the disciples. He said: "O unbelieving generation...how long shall I stay with you? How long shall I put up with you? Bring the boy to me" (Mark 9:19). It's clear from the larger context of Mark 9 that Jesus had already taught the disciples about faith, prayer, casting out demons, and fasting. But when they were unable to put what He taught them into practice, He took the time to teach them again.

This is the kind of commitment it takes to equip people for ministry. Rarely will a person learn how to minister effectively the first time he is taught. Equipping is a process. What's more, people are individuals and need differing amounts of training. Eventually, like the disciples, the people you lead will be able to serve on their own. When they do reach that place of maturity, they will be one step closer to becoming leaders themselves.

This doesn't mean they will need no further coaching. In fact, when Jesus ascended to heaven, He sent the Holy Spirit to convict the world of sin and guide us into all truth. (See John 16:5-15.) The learning process never ends, but it is possible to be adequately prepared for the assignment we have been given.

After I accepted the call to ministry, I wanted to prepare myself for that vocation. So I attended Asbury Theological Seminary in Wilmore, Kentucky, to earn a master's degree in divinity. My training was excellent. I gained biblical depth and spiritual grounding, and I would do it again in a heartbeat. But while I loved my experience at Asbury, I graduated still unprepared for ministry in a number of ways.

I don't fault Asbury for that at all. Some things we learn in a classroom, and some things are better taught on the field. When I entered full-time ministry, I had no idea how to raise serious amounts of money, what to do when a board member was mad at me, how to construct a complex church budget, how to counsel people without getting sued, or how to write sermons every week without spending thirty hours mining Greek and Hebrew texts. This kind of training came from those who worked and served beside me. I learned by doing ministry.

The members of your team need the same kind of equipping from you. They need hands-on training that will enable them to be effective leaders even when you're not around. For some people, this kind of coaching comes easily. For others, especially those who had no mentors themselves, this skill will have to be developed. The good news is that everyone can become better at equipping their team members, especially when they make it a priority. Through the rest of this chapter, I will discuss several strategies to help leaders strengthen their ability to equip their teams. None of these tactics is complicated, but leaders must be intentional about implementing them. Equipping doesn't happen by accident.

CREATE THE RIGHT ENVIRONMENT

Developing an equipping strategy won't do the trick on its own. I know that may seem like an odd thing for me to say. There was a time when I wouldn't have believed that myself, but I have come to realize that it's absolutely true. I once coached a large church in the Atlanta area whose lead pastor is an outstanding communicator. In fact, the ministry is built around his communication gifts.

When the church attempted to launch several training meetings, people simply wouldn't attend. The church tried to institute a new believers' class, and that didn't work either. In a low-key and casual way, one person at a time, the leadership team started asking the congregation why they weren't attending these meetings. The surprising answer was consistently one word, "Why?"

The pastor's teaching was so good and additional training had not been championed or valued for so long the people simply saw no need for it. They believed they could get all they needed from the great sermons they heard during church services. What this congregation needed was not an equipping strategy but a culture shift. No training program can succeed without an awareness of the value of equipping people for ministry, buy-in from the leaders and congregation, and commitment to see the process through for the long haul. You can have the best equipping strategy imaginable, but without an environment that supports it, training efforts will not work.

Before you can begin an equipping program, you must cast vision for the value of this kind of training. I encourage pastors to consider preaching sermons on the importance of becoming an equipping church. Or leaders can address the issue in group meetings. One of the best texts to use is Ephesians 4:11-13:

> It was he who gave some to be apostles, some to be prophets,
> some to be evangelists, and some to be pastors and teachers,
> to prepare God's people for works of service, so that the body
> of Christ may be built up until we all reach unity in the faith
> and in the knowledge of the Son of God and become mature,
> attaining to the whole measure of the fullness of Christ.

Because equipping is connected to the larger value of serving, it is not something that can be relegated to one sermon or staff meeting. For leaders, championing this value is a lifelong process.

The word Paul uses for equipping in Ephesians 4 offers great insight into the essence of this practice. The original Greek word carries the idea of repairing or making whole again, such as mending a fisherman's net or restoring someone to fellowship.[1] The word *equipping* communicates the idea of putting something into the condition it naturally should be in. Equipping is not just about teaching someone how to perform a certain ministry function. It addresses the much larger kingdom idea of serving to grow in maturity and experience fullness in Christ. The beauty of Ephesians 4:11-13 is in the way it highlights the need for the body to work together in "unity" and "in the knowledge of the Son of God."

When a Christian is whole and healthy, serving is seen as a natural part of life, not as a duty. Equipping works best in an environment where the people do not see their service as "helping the pastor get his work done." Ephesians 4 makes it clear that the pastor is helping the people fulfill their call to serve others and build up the body of Christ. When that is understood, training people for specific ministries is a healthy and productive practice.

People want to be successful in what they do. They want to make a difference. They want to know their contribution matters. To accomplish that, they need to become competent and continually work to improve. This is not only true in the marketplace. It's also true in ministry. A volunteer's service is not less valuable because the person is not paid. In fact, their work is actually more valuable because it is a gift.

Different ministry teams will use varying methods to equip their members. For example, the worship and music ministries will likely use rehearsals to accomplish a significant portion of their equipping. But a good rehearsal can become great when the leader understands that the intent of the meeting is not only to prepare for Sunday morning worship. Its purpose is also to help the team members become more mature believers who faithfully and joyfully serve as part of their lifestyle. This can be accomplished by having prayer time, leading a brief devotional, or worshiping for a while before the actual rehearsal. Whatever specific tools your ministry uses, equipping must become a core value because it leads to real effectiveness in ministry.

EQUIPPING IS NOT DEVELOPING

To understand what equipping is, we must know what it is not. Although the two may seem similar, equipping new leaders is not the same as developing them. Those are two separate functions in the leader-building process. Both are vitally important, but one can't be substituted for the other. I will discuss leader development at length in chapter 9. In the meantime, keep these three ideas in mind to distinguish between equipping and developing.

1. Equipping prepares someone to accomplish a specific ministry function or task. Developing invests in someone primarily for his or her personal growth.

The equipping process sets a standard for competency and trains people to get the job done. It is based largely on the purpose, mission, and agenda of the ministry—and it should be. The development process, in contrast, invests primarily in the individual. It typically focuses on cultivating leadership skills, and it adds value to an individual's personal life, not only his role in the church. For example, if a leader wanted to *equip* twenty children's ministry volunteers, he might focus on specific competencies such as how to lead a child to Christ, creative storytelling, and appropriate strategies for discipline (otherwise known as how to say no to a two-year-old without having him bite you, not that I've ever had that happen).

If that leader wanted to *develop* the same twenty children's ministry volunteers, he would need to spend time building them up spiritually as well as teaching and coaching them in leadership. Children's ministry might not even be on the agenda. The process of equipping would help the person become an excellent children's ministry team leader. The process of development would help the person in all areas of life—from getting a raise at work to becoming a better leader at home.

2. Equipping is primarily transactional. Developing is transformational.

A transaction is basically an exchange, and that's a good thing. Most events in our everyday lives are transactional. We stop by a coffee shop on the way to work, give them $1.50, and receive a cup of coffee. We go to work each day and every two weeks receive a paycheck for eighty hours of our time. Those are transactions. In the church, the transaction of equipping looks like this. A person joins the prison ministry team and is thoroughly trained to conduct meaningful ministry to inmates. The training is only for those involved in that ministry. And it is designed to help those team members more effectively fulfill the church's mission to share Christ's love with those in prison. That's an appropriate transaction.

The transformational process, however, is a gift. There is no exchange. When in its purest form, the people on the receiving end of this kind of ministry don't have to do anything to earn transformation. This is what makes it so powerful. When a leader has a pure desire to develop people, she will invest time teaching them great leadership principles just because she wants them to succeed in life, not because she wants them to better serve the church. Equipping can transform people too, but the individuals being transformed are usually those on the receiving end of ministry— the hurting people the church is called to serve. The one who receives the equipping will be impacted by her ministry service. But the more personal impact will come from transformation, which leads to the next point.

> **Equipping prepares people to *do* ministry; developing builds up the people who are *in* ministry.**

3. Equipping changes the ministry. Developing changes the person.

If it is done consistently and well, equipping people for effective ministry will change your church or ministry for the good. Developing the people who serve on your ministry teams will change those individuals for the good. I admit, the value of equipping and developing has a way of blending and blurring. Equipping does build people and developing does prepare people for ministry. The real distinction is this: equipping prepares people to *do* ministry, and developing builds up the people who are *in* ministry. What is most important is that both are at work within your church or ministry.

QUALITIES OF EFFECTIVE TRAINING

If you're like most leaders, you've attended seminars that were incredibly helpful and others that were nearly a complete waste of time. Often the difference is in the instructor leading the training.

Some workshop leaders are great communicators, and others either don't have a good command of the material they're presenting or their delivery is so dry the audience is bored to tears. It is important for leaders to be good communicators, but that is not the only quality that will make them effective at equipping their teams. Even leaders who are gifted teachers won't be effective at equipping people if their training process lacks the following characteristics.

Relevance

Your training must stay current because standards and best practices are constantly changing. Just think how quickly technology has changed. Back in the midnineties, churches hosted websites, but they were not at the center of anyone's ministry. In fact, I focused very little on technology between 1997 and 2001 when I was coaching churches and pastors as vice president of leadership and church development for INJOY.

When I joined the 12Stone Church team in 2001, I still had a midnineties mind-set about website usage. Thankfully, the church was committed to developing its website, and now it is not only a hub for information about the church, but it is also the platform for our online campus, which reaches people all over the world who can't attend our services. I'm still not savvy about websites, but the technology team knows I support what they're doing 100 percent.

Variety

Keep your training interesting by periodically changing the delivery method. Occasionally bring in a guest trainer or a community or business leader to speak to your team. Or invite a pastor from another church in your area to lead a session or two. Perhaps once or twice a year, you may want to use a DVD series to help equip your team, but make sure the content is high-quality and truly meets your training needs.

Practicality

The very nature of equipping demands that it be useful. Reminding the team of the vision is always great, and offering some philosophical background on the need for that area of ministry is a good idea. But ultimately your training must be practical. And though I'm sure you want your team to grow spiritually, you shouldn't feel pressure to make your training sessions Bible studies. The Bible is always relevant, but I have observed too many equipping sessions that devoted hours and hours to studying the Bible and left little or no time for actual ministry training. God's Word will not return void, but it may not address the specific skills your team will need to be effective in a particular area of ministry. One of the most practical things a leader can do is to offer hands-on training as part of the equipping process.

Inspiration

Practical doesn't mean boring! The training should stir and challenge those who attend. Vision is important and will help motivate the team, but stories of changed lives will go even further to inspire them. Share stories about people on the team and the individuals they have served. This will remind the team that they are making an impact. Keeping the training fun and light will also go a long way to encourage your team. They are busy people with plenty of everyday stress and burdens. If you can lighten their load by making them laugh or smile while equipping them, you will have hit a home run!

Focus

I know it can be challenging to gather new and existing team members to training meetings. And, of course, that makes it tempting to add other items to the agenda while you have everyone in one room. This may seem like an efficient use of time, but it's actually counterproductive. Even ministry times can be out of place during training sessions. I was in a training meeting for ushers and greeters once, and the pastor decided to take time to pray for and commission a group of missionaries leaving the next day. It threw the meeting completely off point. Announcements, reminders, and general ministry housekeeping unnecessarily prolong the training time and truly detract from the overall quality of the equipping program. Keep it simple. Stay focused, train your team with world-class excellence, then let the people go home! This is how you will get them to come back for the next training session.

Plan for Success

You've probably heard the saying, "If you fail to plan, then you plan to fail." Equipping is no different. You must adequately prepare before you begin your training process in order for it to be successful. Through years of coaching pastors, I have identified several items leaders should think about before they begin their equipping process. These tips are basic, but if any are left out, the entire process will suffer.

Do your best to connect the right person with the right ministry.

Sometimes this comes up during the invitation process we talked about in chapter 5. But you'd be surprised how often this surfaces after a person has joined a ministry team. Recently I had a conversation with someone involved in a local food cooperative.

When I asked him how he ended up in that area of ministry, he said, "Well, Joe said there was a great need, and I said I'd help. But I don't enjoy it. I really want to develop men in small groups."

The pressure to meet an immediate ministry need can easily cause leaders to put the wrong person in a ministry role. It's true that people with the spiritual gifts of helps or service can do well in several different ministries. But it is also true that nearly everyone is best suited to one or two ministry areas. Spiritual gifts tests, talking about passions and interests, and inviting someone to participate in a ministry with the understanding that they are experimenting for a short time are all great ways to help them find the right spot on a ministry team.

Determine the desired results for each ministry.

What do you want the ministry to accomplish? If you don't ask this question, you won't get the results you want. Great equipping starts with a clear understanding of the goals for that ministry. Take small group ministry for example. If the desired result is to improve participants' Bible knowledge, the equipping process will train small group leaders to take people deep into the Word. If the desired result is to form a relational connection and provide pastoral care, your training will go in another direction. If your desire is to change lives, that will put yet another slant on your equipping process.

In one church I was coaching, the leaders focused on helping their small group leaders become strong Bible teachers. When they began to discuss what they really wanted for their small groups, they discovered their goal was to make them much more interactive. That greatly changed the direction of their training. Instead of preparing the small group leaders to become Bible teachers, they trained them to become application-oriented discussion leaders. And the change produced the church's desired results.

Identify the skills and core competencies needed to achieve your desired results.

Knowing which skills are needed to achieve your goals will have the most critical impact on the direction your training program takes. I'll refer again to the example of the church that realized it wanted its small groups to be more interactive. Because the small group leaders needed to be application-oriented discussion leaders rather than Bible teachers, the training had to focus on topics such as how to write and ask great questions, and how to lead focused and robust discussions. It also needed to emphasize using good study materials instead of teaching skills. All of the training moved in the direction of building the core competencies that would enable the small group leaders to facilitate application-oriented and, ultimately, life-changing discussions.

Consider the cultural and philosophical biases of your church.

Every region has cultural distinctives, and they get even more specific when you move to the state and city level. In Southern California, where I'm from, college football is not the center of life. But in the Southeast, it's like a cult. The rivalry between the University of Alabama Crimson Tide and the Auburn University Tigers is scary. And the Georgia Bulldog fans are simply not to be messed with! College football is so big, in fact, that game schedules affect Saturday evening church attendance in a big way.

Churches too have unique cultural dynamics. We can pretend they don't, but the wise thing would be to acknowledge the reality we minister in and carry that awareness into the design of our training processes. If a church, for example, has a casual culture, the training should have the same feel. Philosophical biases matter too. For instance, denominational churches have specific governing structures that shape how teams and committees are empowered. If you're part of a denominational church, you should carry its governing philosophy into the way you organize your training process so there is alignment throughout the teams and ministries.

Be prepared to invest in the necessary training materials and tools.

It's amazing how creative a person can be with modest resources. I'm a fan of any church that demonstrates great stewardship. Yet a certain level of investment is needed, at least at a baseline level, to provide good tools and training for your teams. After you beg, borrow, and steal all you can (OK, don't literally steal),

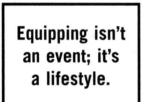

Equipping isn't an event; it's a lifestyle.

you must find room in the church budget for training expenses and the equipment needed to accomplish your goals. And when it comes to training, less is more. It's better to provide well for fewer ministries than to provide inadequately for several ministries. If you are not sure what your teams need, ask them. They know!

EQUIPPING IS AN ONGOING PROCESS

Any leader who is serious about equipping knows training requires more than offering a few classes then assuming your team is set for life. I suppose that would work if the ministry never changed, the church never grew, or the culture stayed the same. But that's not reality. Equipping is a continual process. Successful people know they can never stop learning, and the same is true in ministry.

We should be constantly growing and becoming more effective at reaching those around us.

As leaders, it is our responsibility to encourage our teams to keep growing, to never think they have "arrived." Equipping isn't an event; it's a lifestyle. The following tips, if practiced consistently, will help you make equipping part of the life of your church instead of a special focus for a season.

Communicate often with your teams about desired results.

The purpose of equipping ministry teams is twofold—to give team members an opportunity to grow spiritually by serving others and to see actual ministry results. You don't want one without the other. It's never wise to lower your standards by allowing an ineffective team to continue. This hurts not only the church but also the people on the team. One of the most practical ways to stay on top of a team's effectiveness is to regularly discuss the progress they are making. Ask simple, direct questions such as, What is working? What's not working? How can we improve? Then incorporate what you learn into your training process.

Give generous amounts of praise and affirmation.

Earlier in this chapter I noted that the original Greek word for equipping carried the idea of mending and making whole, or to make again as it was originally intended to be. God wants the individuals on your church teams to be built up, encouraged, and loved to a place where consistent serving becomes a lifestyle. This builds the body of Christ and advances God's kingdom. The simple act of saying thank you and telling your team they are doing a good job can literally change eternity. Think about it. As you build them up, they build the ministry up, the ministry changes lives, and eternity is impacted!

Provide ongoing training.

A great equipping process includes continued training, but don't make it complicated. Your ushers team, for example, will do fine with a couple of one- or two-hour huddles twice a year after their initial training. Your small group leaders can do very well with three or four "Lunch and Learn" sessions a year after their initial training. In both examples, it's important to choose current and relevant topics, and design a meeting that is inspiring, engaging, practical, and interactive. It's also important to let the teams have fun and provide creative ways for them to get to know one another better.

Check for fruit and joy.

This is where the rubber meets the road. Periodically you should ask your team a simple but important question. It is best to do this one on one, perhaps over a cup of coffee, but you could also do this with a small group. Ask those on the team what fruit (results) and joys they are experiencing in the ministry team. The ministry must have both. Results without joy is drudgery, and no one can or should endure that for long. Joy without results may be fun for a while, but ultimately it will be just as frustrating that the team's efforts are not paying off. Periodically asking about those two areas will give you helpful insights about the people on your team. And it will teach you ways to build them up and improve your ministry.

It is impossible to amplify your leadership without building a great team. This means we must learn to invite people into meaningful ministry with sincerity and conviction. Then, when our team is in place, we must train them for effective service.

AMPLIFY YOUR LEADERSHIP

Establish a Relationship	→	Engage a Follower	→	Embrace a Team Member	→	Coach an Apprentice	→	Mentor a New Leader

• *Connect* at the heart • *Appreciate* people for who they are	• *Encourage* people to bring out their best • *Inspire* people to follow the vision	• *Invite* individuals into meaningful ministry • *Equip* team members for ministry success		

As the above illustration shows, the fourth stage in the leadership development process is to coach an apprentice. This is where the process becomes exponentially more rewarding because we will identify and work with emerging leaders. Coaching aspiring leaders is challenging, but it is so much fun! Two skills will empower you to be an excellent coach—knowing which apprentice to *select* and how to *include* that individual in meaningful ministry.

PART

FOUR

COACH AN APPRENTICE

It is a noble thing to prepare the way for someone
who might surpass you in leadership.

Donald Trump's popular TV show *The Apprentice* first aired in 2004 and gained a whopping 28 million viewers by the season finale.[1] The show divided eight men and eight women into two teams and assigned them a different task each week. The projects pit one team against the other, and the winners received a luxurious prize. The losing team, however, was sent to the boardroom, where Mr. Trump would decide which contestant would hear his now-iconic pronouncement, "You're fired!" The last person standing would be declared the apprentice.

Bill Rancic was the winner the first year, and he continues to enjoy a thriving career. Bill was already an entrepreneur when he competed on the show, but his life was forever changed after he was chosen as the apprentice. That's really the point of the show. All the drama is about the fifteen who will be fired, but the show's real purpose is to select the right person to join the Trump organization.

Trump is a savvy businessman, and he knows that choosing the right apprentice will affect the future of his empire. He hires only one person a year via national television, but he hires many people throughout the year in boardrooms without cameras and crews. If "The Donald" were here to talk with us, I'm sure he'd say that his leaders determine his destiny. I know that's true of ministries, especially the local church.

Moses also understood the importance of choosing the right apprentice. Joshua was very young when Moses selected him as his aid (Num. 11:28). Joshua grew to be a strong leader under Moses's tutelage and eventually became one of twelve men selected to explore Canaan, the Promised Land (Num. 13:1-8). One person was chosen from each tribe, and Joshua was selected as the leader from the tribe of Ephraim.

Donald Trump and Moses are clearly very different leaders, but they do share at least one similarity. They both knew they couldn't reach their goals alone. They needed apprentice leaders.

I can't speak for Trump, but it is clear in Scripture that Moses invited God into the selection process. He knew what we as ministry leaders must also realize: that we don't select completely on our own. Yes, we need skills to make good choices, but as spiritual leaders we pray and ask God for guidance. In Joshua 1, we see the huge role God had in Joshua's leadership after the death of Moses.

After the death of Moses the servant of the LORD, the LORD said to Joshua son of Nun, Moses' aide: "Moses my servant is dead. Now then, you and all these people, get ready to cross the Jordan River into the land I am about to give to them— to the Israelites. I will give you every place where you set your foot, as I promised Moses. Your territory will extend from the desert to Lebanon, and from the great river, the Euphrates—all the Hittite country—to the Great Sea on the west. No one will be able to stand up against you all the days of your life. As I was with Moses, so I will be with you; I will never leave you nor forsake you. Be strong and courageous, because you will lead these people to inherit the land I swore to their forefathers to give them."

—JOSHUA 1:1-6

The interesting thing about the apprentice process, whether it is Joshua or Bill Rancic, is that not everyone is chosen. It's not a popularity contest, and it should not be politically influenced. There were many great people in Moses's army, and there are impressive people in Trump's organization, but only a few will rise to become leaders. This is why the selection process is so important. Part of the responsibility falls on the potential apprentice and what he or she is willing to do to be noticed. And part of it is up to the leader making the decision. I have to believe it didn't go unnoticed that of the twelve who spied out the land of Canaan, Joshua and Caleb were the only ones who gave a positive report. (See Numbers 13.)

In the big picture, the apprentice process never ends. When Joshua became the leader of Israel, he began selecting apprentices from among the next generation. I often tell our 12Stone ministry team that I don't represent the future. I'm part of the future in that I help set the direction the church will move in and build toward it.

But ultimately it's the next generation who will lead the way. It's my job to develop leadership skills in younger staff members so they can increasingly take the reigns of leadership.

This is one of the reasons I'm so excited about our intern program. We are investing in the future leadership of 12Stone and other churches! The interns and other young staff are our apprentices, and we know how important their development is to their future and the church's.

Let me make this more personal. I was chosen, and it changed my life. John Maxwell selected me to join the Skyline Wesleyan Church team as an intern in 1982. That first year was a wild ride. I discovered how much I didn't know about leadership. This was a shock to my system because from my late high school years through college I had been "in charge." Even during seminary, I was the president of the senior class and had the privilege of delivering the graduating address that year.

I'm not saying I was completely worthless as a leader back then, but I was close. I learned that a person can be smart, hardworking, and passionate about God, but that alone doesn't make him a good leader. He may even have great people intuition. That's good, but it's not enough. Leaders must know how to lead. I didn't when I started out, at least not very well. I desperately needed someone to coach, shape, and guide me as a leader. I needed someone to select me as an apprentice.

At the close of my year as an intern, I had learned much but still had a long way to go. John invited me to remain on staff and become one of his young apprentices. That opportunity changed my life and resulted in twenty years of ministry together and a friendship that is still strong today. This is the heart of *Amplified*

Leadership, and I want to keep the leadership baton moving forward by handing it off to others through leadership training.

This idea carries over to the dozens, or hundreds, of potential leaders who volunteer in your church or ministry organization. They are waiting to be selected as apprentice leaders and given the opportunity to learn from your leadership. Doug Franks was one of those young volunteers at 12Stone.

Doug was part of the greeters ministry when the church drew about twenty-five hundred people each weekend. At that time there were about thirty greeters on the team, and Doug and his wife, Jill, served at the Sunday evening service. Soon Pastor Mark Eiken spotted Doug's leadership potential, and he and Pastor Chris Huff began to consistently invest in Doug's leadership development. It began with Mark essentially saying, "I'll lead. You watch and learn." That eventually progressed to, "You lead. I'll watch and coach."

The coaching from Mark and Chris has spanned everything from personal calling and marriage to strategic leadership and identifying new leaders. Today, as 12Stone draws more than ten thousand people each weekend, Doug oversees our entire greeter ministry, which has about three hundred people on the team. Doug manages it, and Mark contributes when needed. Doug makes key decisions every weekend. Although Doug is not a full-time church employee, he is as influential as some staff members.

Who is rising to the top in your church or on your ministry team? Who are you considering for leadership? Are you praying that God will bring leaders to your church? Are you asking God to show you the future leaders He has in mind? Do you keep a list of names? Who will be the next apprentice you select? In many ways, your leadership is limited only to your ability to develop more leaders.

Leadership development isn't flashy or fast, but it will change the church forever. Leadership development isn't about increasing your attendance in the next few months. It's an intentional and methodical process that takes time. It's about strengthening your church and positioning it for significantly increased and sustainable growth.

My number one priority and passion is too see more people following Jesus. But second to that, I'm most fired up about developing new leaders. It's powerful to see someone chosen and then to grow as a leader. It's even more powerful to see that new leader impact the ministry in such a way that more people say yes to Jesus. Again, that's the bottom line. The real reason for investing so much time and effort into developing new leaders is so we can reach more people for Christ!

Chapter Seven

SELECT THE BEST POTENTIAL LEADERS

When you select the right apprentice, the mentoring relationship
will benefit both the individual and the ministry.

Jesus selected a team of twelve leaders, but out of that group He chose three to invest even more time into. Peter, James, and John were the ones Jesus invited to join Him in the Garden of Gethsemane, and they witnessed His transfiguration. Of the three, John was closest to Jesus, but each of those men made a profound impact on the kingdom. Peter preached the gospel with boldness and led countless thousands to follow Christ. James was the first to be martyred for the sake of the gospel, and it was John who received the prophetic vision recorded in the Book of Revelation.

We'd all like to have Peter, James, and John as leaders on our team. Jesus clearly trusted them to spread the message of His kingdom, and they didn't let Him down. Jesus chose well to say the least.

You might be thinking, "Yeah, but He's God!" That's true, but Jesus knew how it felt to be disappointed with one of His followers. After all, Judas was on Jesus's team. I'm not saying Jesus made a mistake by choosing Judas, but that decision caused Him pain. Most, if not all, leaders have been disappointed at some point in the people they chose as leaders. I'm sure you can think of a few people right now you wish you'd never selected for leadership.

Choosing the right people wasn't only important to Jesus. It was also important to the early church. When church members began complaining (imagine that!), the apostles stepped up to the plate to solve the problem. In Acts 6, we see that they took great care to select the right individuals to simply wait tables.

> In those days when the number of disciples was increasing, the Grecian Jews among them complained against the Hebraic Jews because their widows were being overlooked in the daily distribution of food. So the Twelve gathered all the disciples together and said, "It would not be right for us to neglect the ministry of the word of God in order to wait on tables. Brothers, choose seven men from among you who are known to be full of the Spirit and wisdom. We will turn this responsibility over to them and will give our attention to prayer and the ministry of the word."
>
> This proposal pleased the whole group. They chose Stephen, a man full of faith and of the Holy Spirit; also Philip, Procorus, Nicanor, Timon, Parmenas, and Nicolas from Antioch, a convert to Judaism. They presented these

men to the apostles, who prayed and laid their hands on them. So the word of God spread. The number of disciples in Jerusalem increased rapidly, and a large number of priests became obedient to the faith.

—Acts 6:1-7

The disciples gave careful and intentional consideration to who would be chosen. We know that those selected were full of the Holy Spirit and wisdom. We know they did not all share the same gifts. Stephen, for instance, was full of faith. The important result is seen in verse 7. The Word of God spread. The number of disciples grew quickly. The church continued to advance! More people followed Jesus. A large number of priests became obedient to the faith. The church became stronger! This is what the process of leadership development is all about—building the church!

SELECTING THE RIGHT APPRENTICE

If you're anything like me, you'll be encouraged to know that Jesus did not choose leaders because they were perfect. He looked for people with potential and who would help Him fulfill His purpose on the earth. Ultimately, this is what should drive us as we select potential leaders. But through the years I have seen leaders make three common mistakes when selecting an apprentice.

Making a decision based on politics

This happens more often than most leaders care to admit. There are churches and ministries that experience little to no political pressure, but they are rare. Whether they would ever use the term *political* or not, most pastors have experienced relational pressure that got so intense, they selected someone for leadership they wouldn't otherwise have chosen. I have.

After launching the Joshua's Men leadership development program I mentioned earlier, I caved in to relational pressure on two occasions. In both cases I placed men in the group who I didn't think were right for the program. And in both situations that decision proved to be a big mistake. The first time was when a young man's wife came to see me. She was upset that her husband had never been selected to participate in the program. She listed all of his great abilities and his years of service to the church, and then threw in that he was a big financial giver!

She spent nearly an hour making her case and influencing me to her way of thinking. Yes, I wimped out. I put her husband in the group. He wasn't ready, and the group suffered. In the second case, I had selected a sharp young guy but not his best friend. These two men were nearly inseparable and truly did have a great friendship. I knew, however, that one was right for Joshua's Men and the other wasn't. But yes, I gave in to the pressure again, and the group suffered. In neither case was the yearlong experience ruined. But I know the men in the program didn't receive all they might have. Whether it is choosing an apprentice or another issue in ministry, allowing politics to influence your decisions is a costly mistake in leadership.

Underestimating a person's capacity

It is easy to miss the possibilities that lie within an individual. Talent and ability are not always obvious. The young shepherd David is a good example. When Saul was looking for someone to fight Goliath, David was completely overlooked. Yet in the end, David was the one who killed Israel's greatest enemy.

Although most of us would like to think we can spot hidden potential, it is more common for a leader to underestimate someone's capacity than to overestimate it. Most leaders are in a hurry, so they assess situations quickly and move on unless something jumps out at them right away. But that is how we miss so much.

There are a few leaders who move too slowly. But that is far less common if for no other reason than because the demands of ministry keep you moving fast. When an organization is hiring for a new job, the leaders take great care to choose the right person. They have multiple conversations in a number of settings with several candidates to ultimately decide on one individual. They take their time because it's too easy to miss something important.

There is something within the human nature that often assumes less about someone than more. We don't usually take the time to look closely to see a person's potential. We want people ready to perform like an old pro on day one, and that's just not how things work. Most people have to be nurtured to function at their best.

My son, John-Peter, is a good guitar player, but he didn't start out that way. If his guitar teacher had judged him based on his ability and overall capacity at the beginning, he could have easily overlooked how well John-Peter would be able to play one day. Fortunately his guitar instructors looked beyond the surface, and they saw his talent and capacity for great musicianship. The same kind of great care and vision for people is also needed when we are selecting potential leaders!

Making assumptions of any kind

Judging a book by its cover is not a good idea with a book and definitely not with people. Jesus chose some of the most unlikely people to lead the early church. From a loud and brash fisherman to a proud and scheming tax collector, the people Jesus chose are individuals you and I easily might have passed over because of our assumptions about them.

Assumptions are easy to make. We judge people based on what they do, how they look, how much they earn, whom they married, what level of education they have, where they live, how they dress, what music they like, how they talk, and the list goes on. The dangerous thing about assumptions is that we are often wrong. How often have you assumed a person would be too busy or not interested in taking on a leadership role? In my experience, the people we thought would be unavailable were actually honored, if not blown away, that we selected them to move into a leadership position. My hunch is that you have had similar experiences.

> **Good leaders look with eyes of faith and use discernment when choosing potential leaders.**

Good leaders look with eyes of faith and use discernment when choosing potential leaders. They don't rely solely on things that can be seen. As leaders it is good for us to use common wisdom. But it's also important that we allow the Holy Spirit to show us things we can't see with our natural eyes and help us resist the temptation to assume. My challenge to you is twofold. First, reflect on the most common assumptions you make about people. And second, make a concerted effort to stop allowing those assumptions to influence your decisions.

DISCERNING CHARACTER IN AN APPRENTICE

As a wise leader, you'll want to become a "discerner of potential." Discerning leaders want to know a person's heart first, then determine his ability. Obviously, it can be difficult to know what is in someone's heart, but asking the following questions will help you discern potential leaders' character.

Will they follow?

Good apprentices demonstrate a willingness to follow. This gives great insight into their attitude. We were eager to have Jason Berry join our staff at 12Stone. In his previous church he carried a significant responsibility as the associate pastor. But he was a young leader stepping into a megachurch environment for the first time, so we challenged Jason to serve on our children's ministry team. At first this idea was a stretch for Jason, but he quickly understood the big-picture vision and was willing to follow our leadership for a season of development. Jason embraced the importance of the children's ministry and served with his whole heart on that team. His leadership proved to be outstanding, but more importantly, he served with a great attitude. Today Jason is the pastor of our Flowery Branch campus! A great attitude coupled with great leadership opens doors and opportunities. This idea is true for all volunteer leaders. They must have a great attitude and be willing to follow before they can lead!

Will they serve?

Good apprentices exhibit a willingness to serve. This gives insight into their heart. Stephen Cohen is one of 12Stone's great volunteer leaders. He and his wife, Christine, are a wonderful couple who love to serve. The Cohens served on the spiritual formation team at the Central campus and were involved in a small groups ministry for new Christians. When we decided to start a new campus on Saturday night, we asked the Cohens to make a pretty big change. We invited Stephen to lead the usher team. That's a far cry from teaching in a small group setting! But Stephen jumped right in, and we immediately saw that his heart was to serve, not simply to lead in one area of ministry. After a short while, we were able to move him so he could once again teach and guide new Christians, but he remained part of the Saturday campus. Similar to being willing to follow before they lead, apprentices must have a heart to serve.

Will they learn?

Good apprentices display a willingness to learn. This gives insight into their ego. No one wants to follow someone who thinks he knows it all. I attended the Catalyst 2010 Conference at the Gwinnett Arena here in Atlanta and talked with several leaders there. They were all great guys, but something struck me when one of them said, "Yeah, I come to hang out, but I don't go inside to hear the talks. I've heard all that stuff before." Wow. Really? That's like saying, "I've read the Bible before, and I have all that down now!" Scary! I don't make it into every session at Catalyst, but I'm certain I don't know all "that stuff." And I love listening to the CDs after the conference. A good leader is able to tame his or her ego enough to keep on learning. Leaders are readers and lifelong learners.

Will they sacrifice?

Good apprentices demonstrate a willingness to sacrifice. This gives insight into their perspective about life. I mentioned previously that I traveled to Sri Lanka after the tsunami hit in 2004, and Norwood Davis accompanied me. (Of course, Norwood would say I traveled with him. And he did prove to be the Indiana Jones of the trip—Norwood will eat anything!) What I haven't told you is that somewhere in the middle of that little country, as Norwood and I talked about the possibility of him joining our team at 12Stone, I brought up the very important subject of his salary. Norwood came from the business community, where he earned a very substantial salary, something far more than we could offer. I will never forget what he said: "Dan, it really doesn't matter what you pay me because God has told me to do this." In an instant, I saw his willingness to sacrifice and fully understood his perspective on life and eternity. This beautiful spirit is seen in all good leaders, whether they are paid or volunteer.

Will they be honest?

Great apprentices are honest. This gives insight into their level of maturity. Honesty is such a basic concept, yet for many it is difficult to achieve. I'm not referring to someone who actually lies. I'm talking about people who simply can't get past their personal insecurities and break through to authenticity. These individuals will not experience enough maturity to lead. They will need time to become self-aware enough to be real with others. This is easier to discern than it may seem. The first sign is whether they are comfortable simply being who they are.

DISCERNING ABILITY IN AN APPRENTICE

After discerning the heart issues, you'll need to look for more measurable qualities, namely their personal abilities. Keep in mind that in both character and competency, you are not looking for someone who has "arrived." You do need to spot talent, but you are also looking for potential.

Competence

Competence measures what a person is currently good at. Like mining for gold, discovering a person's ability is not easy because it's not always found in the obvious places. Most people look to an individual's profession to determine his core competencies. We want to know what he does and how well he does it. That is important. Obviously, you want to select people who are good at what they do. But, again, because you are looking for potential, keep in mind that the person might not be a star yet but rather a diamond in the rough. Further, if the individual is in the wrong job or has poor leadership above him, it may be difficult for him to flourish. You can sometimes discover what a person is good at from his hobbies. In some cases, the person's avocation should be his vocation! The bottom line here is that you are looking for men and women who are good at something!

Capacity

Capacity involves a person's ability to stretch and grow beyond his or her current level. Life and leadership are finite propositions. Everyone eventually hits a lid. It may be because the individual lacks drive, talent, and training. Or it may be that he just ran out of time. With that said, one of the things that separates the good from the great is that the great clearly have a higher capacity to stretch and grow for the next season. These are the people you want to select. Choosing someone who can only lead a ministry as it is does not help you, and it will frustrate the person you select. You need someone who can move the ministry to the next level. Capacity, like all the qualities I've mentioned, can be difficult to discern and assess. Don't let that stop you. You will get better the more you practice.

> **Great potential leaders have a capacity to stretch and grow for the next season.**

Energy

Leaders have drive. They bring energy into the mix. They don't wait or hold back. They jump in and take initiative. You want to choose apprentices who are content, or learning to be content, at a heart level but are never satisfied as leaders. By "never satisfied," I don't mean that they are unappreciative and never happy. I mean that they want to make things happen. The Bible tells us to be content in our current circumstance. (See Philippians 4:10-12; 1 Timothy 6:5-9.) But that doesn't mean we should be complacent about the future. That's not the nature of a leader. Leaders push for progress. I can personally say that I am a content person. I am content with who I am and the life God has given me. But I'm not satisfied that the church I lead has reached its potential, and I put considerable energy toward its continued growth. This is the trait you are looking for.

Relational skills

You know people who are relational blockheads. They have the people skills of a two-by-four piece of pine. Dale Carnegie can't help them, and neither can you. Jesus loves them, and they can serve somewhere on the team, but you don't need to select them for leadership. It doesn't matter how smart or faithful they are, people who don't have a natural ability to get along with and understand others will struggle as leaders. It is not imperative that they have finesse and a highly polished relational intuition. But if they don't have some basic people skills, you are headed for trouble. The key to a person's ability to develop in this area is his own awareness of his relational savvy. Reviewing the *connect* and *appreciate* skills discussed in Part One will give you a clear picture of what it takes to be a relational leader.

Intelligence

This is a sensitive one, but I have to put it on the list. God can use a donkey if He wants to, but let's be honest. You don't see a lot of donkeys in leadership. So let me be blunt; great leaders are smart people. They may not be intellectuals or have high academic performance. In fact, it's often practical wisdom combined with an ability to reason that give leaders the edge. Great leaders don't need an IQ that is through the roof, but if everyone else thinks faster, deeper, and more clearly than they do, again, leadership will be difficult. You can discern a great deal about a person's intelligence by the questions he asks and the solutions he provides. Asking someone to tell you about the last problem he faced and how he solved it will reveal a lot.

SPIRITUAL LEADERSHIP REQUIRES A HEART FOR GOD

King David was an imperfect leader, but he had a heart for God. I'm sure we can all relate to that. We are imperfect leaders pursuing a perfect God, on mission according to His purpose and glory. No matter what our capability, ministry leaders must have a love for God. We all know of David's failings, but his passion for God can't be ignored. Psalm 63 gives us a great picture of his heart for God.

> O God, you are my God, earnestly I seek you; my soul thirsts for you, my body longs for you, in a dry and weary land where there is no water. I have seen you in the sanctuary and beheld your power and your glory. Because your love is better than life, my lips will glorify you. I will praise you as long as I live, and in your name I will lift up my hands. My soul will be satisfied as with the richest of foods; with singing lips my mouth will praise you.
>
> —PSALM 63:1-5

You can choose an apprentice who is young in his walk with Jesus if that person is passionate about his spiritual journey. In fact, I'd rather have an apprentice who is young in his faith and diligently pursuing God than a seasoned believer who has grown cool in his love of God. The time allowed for apprenticing can be short. In fact, if we're really honest, it can overlap with on-the-job equipping and developing. (We'll hit developing in chapter 9.) That's not ideal, but it's the reality. Don't get hung up on that. I applaud you for equipping and developing your team. Don't worry if your time lines aren't perfect!

Because you likely will have only a short time with your apprentice, you probably will not want to choose a new Christian to groom as a new leader. But someone still relatively young in his or her faith development is a fine candidate. Another thing to consider is the level of responsibility the person will have. The more responsibility the person will have, the longer the apprenticeship should be. Apprenticeship is loosely defined as a period of time devoted to significant training. Full empowerment comes later. (We will discuss empowerment in chapter 10.)

The beautiful thing about pursuing God is that we will always "catch" Him! The truth is, God is pursuing us! I love the story of the prodigal son in Luke 15. It paints such a vivid picture of the Father's heart for His children. When the lost son returns, the father runs out to meet him. There are no questions, and there is no punishment, only a party. His son came home! This is the heart of the Father who longs for and loves each of His children. The power in this, for our context, is that any leader who will pursue God will find Him and be found by Him.

If a leader is intimate with the Father, it will be easy to see. The result of this dual pursuit and connection with God is that ordinary people end up doing extraordinary things. I know this is true for me. I'm a quintessential late bloomer and pretty ordinary in most ways. Yet God has allowed me to be part of what has been unquestionably extraordinary in His church. It's easy for me to recognize and acknowledge achievement in ministry because it's ultimately not my doing. It is God's Spirit in operation and His kindness at work.

I trust that's true for you too. You are gifted and talented, but ultimately it is God at work within you that enables you to accomplish what you do for the kingdom. Knowing that truth makes leadership, with both the successes and failures, so much easier to understand. And it better prepares you to coach an apprentice. So when you encounter ordinary people doing extraordinary things because they pursue God, remember that these are the kind of people you want to select as apprentice leaders.

JUMP IN!

Whether you have selected one apprentice for a specific ministry or several to serve in a variety of areas, don't wait to include them. Jump in right away.

Put your whole heart into it.

When it comes to leadership development, you will reap what you invest. If you want 100 percent from the apprentice leader, you need to pour 100 percent of yourself into the process. Perhaps you're thinking, "I've been giving 100 percent all the way through this process." That's good. Don't stop. Most leaders end their investment after the equipping phase, and this is where the greatest impact begins. Continue the process through to inclusion, development, and empowerment. The never-ending need for more leaders will make you want to "recruit and run." Fight that temptation! If you do that, you'll break the cycle and will never complete the leadership development process.

Though the potential leader you selected may show great promise, if he doesn't receive the needed inclusion, development, and empowerment, he will flounder and is much more likely to quit. If you invest deeply in him, the new leader will not only do well, but also he is much more likely to love what he's doing and continue in ministry.

Recognize and accept the risk.

It is obvious but worth saying that no choice you make is foolproof. People are people. Some leaders you choose will not work out. Don't let that paralyze you or cause you to overthink each leadership choice. I encourage you to give people the benefit of the doubt, especially when the choices are close but unclear. If you believe in the person, he or she will likely surprise you and rise to the occasion. Yes, it's a risk. I've had some major blowouts through the years. Some people just weren't who I thought they were and couldn't do the job. Others were very gifted but misused their authority. Don't let that hold you back. Take the risk and jump in.

Develop the relationship.

It doesn't matter if you have ten leaders to coach or one hundred. They all need to sense and experience genuine relational connection. If you have many leaders to lead, you will need to create organizational layers so other leaders can help you. However you structure those layers, it is essential that the relationship is warm and vibrant. Not only does this make leading more enjoyable, but the potential leaders will also stay with you longer. What's more, they will eventually replicate with others what you have invested in them.

Be clear about expectations.

Apprenticeships are designed for learning. It is not appropriate to make the potential leader read your mind or play guessing games. Spell everything out clearly. If you are like me, you prefer to cast vision, develop relationships, and empower people. You like to inspire the emerging leaders and turn them loose. That's fun, but it will backfire on you before long if you stop there. You need to spell out in detail what level of commitment you expect and exactly which responsibilities you are assigning to them. Do this in writing, but try to strike a balance. You don't want to micromanage them to make sure they satisfy all the items on your list. You want the list to set them free because it has made your expectations clear!

Press toward measurable change.

Part of clearly communicating your expectations is making known the changes you want to see in two areas—in the leader and in the ministry. The first is the most important. In fact, the apprentice's personal growth is so important I will devote chapter 9 to exploring this topic. In short, you need to identify specific areas of growth for the emerging leader. Keep the lists short and positive by focusing on cultivating the person's strengths. Also set understandable, practical, and measurable goals for the apprentice to achieve in the ministry. Growth equals change!

Have the tough conversations.

At 12Stone we call it the last 10 percent. This is the part of the conversation that is tough to have. It's the part that can put butterflies in your stomach. It is also where the real issues are addressed, the ones that can bring significant life change. If you want to lead well and develop leaders, you must have these difficult conversations.

The last 10 percent should not be motivated by anger or frustration. The talk may not even be about a serious problem. What your apprentice needs is for you to speak real truth, even if it's uncomfortable in the moment. The leader needs you to get to the real heart of the matter, to the issues that are preventing him from being the best leader possible. The leaders you coach depend on you for this. These conversations won't happen often, but when they do, they will be game changers!

Choosing an apprentice is only the first part of the coaching process. Just as important as finding the right individual is actually giving them opportunities to serve. They need the chance to get in the trenches and do real ministry. Read on and I'll show you how to truly *include* emerging leaders in real ministry.

Chapter Eight

INCLUDE EMERGING LEADERS

Giving apprentices real responsibility allows them
to experience the reality of leadership.

WHEN I WAS in my late teens, I played basketball in a city league in my hometown of San Diego. My team wasn't very good, but I still found myself on the bench most of the time. If Coach Jerry did let me play, it usually was only during the last few minutes because we were getting killed anyway. I remember once asking Coach Jerry which position he preferred me to play, forward or guard, and he said, "It doesn't matter."

That didn't stop me, though. I never missed a practice. I gave it everything I had, and I'm proud to say I usually dropped at least one ball through the net. I loved to play, and I hated sitting on the bench. Leaders are the same way. They don't like the bench. Granted, basketball is different from ministry, but the passion to be included is the same. I wasn't a great player as a teenager, but I knew one thing for sure. I would never get better on the bench.

Your apprentice leaders are the same way. They need game time. They need to be included. They need to know you trust them and believe in them, which are both core to empowering leaders. From this point on, you'll find that there is a lot of overlap in the leadership development process. When you include your apprentices, they begin leading. While they are leading, you are developing and empowering them, skills I will discuss at length in Part Five.

For the sake of clarity I have divided this process into five practices and ten specific skills. But the more you engage in this leadership process, the more you will see that it is not linear. It is not black and white. The art of developing leaders is colorful, and the lines are not straight. When these concepts are lived out, the process of including, developing, and empowering new leaders is fluid. I have put them in this sequence to clearly communicate the qualities needed to develop leaders.

But let me be clear. You do need all of the components and skills I discuss in this book. If you leave any out, the leadership development process will break down quickly. Think of it like a football playbook. Most of the time you will follow the calls and plays as they are written in the book. That's foundational to success. But it is not uncommon to call an audible during a critical point in the game. In the context of building leaders, an audible is called most often in the inclusion, developing, and empowerment parts of the process.

In this chapter, however, we will focus on inclusion. In the same way I was asked to sit on the bench in high school more than the star players were, you will use your top leaders for greater responsibilities. Simply put, you will include some leaders more than others. Jesus did. Remember how close He was to Peter, James, and John? He drew them aside more often than the others. But all the disciples were included. Jesus intentionally gave each of them a chance to get in the game. You must do the same as a developer of leaders.

I assume the best of you as a leader. I assume that you are not protecting your turf. I trust that you are not protecting your social and emotional territory. I assume that you do not work out of the principle of scarcity, which leads to exclusion. This prevents emerging leaders from rising to significant leadership. A friend once told me a story about a senior pastor who literally drew a ten-foot circle around the pulpit in his church. Each time someone joined the team, the pastor took the new staff member onto the platform, pointed to the circle, and said, "You don't ever go inside the circle. That area is reserved for me."

That guy is the poster pastor for what *not* to do. Insecurity can wreck any leader. Your ministry no doubt has very talented leaders. They may be on the board, on the staff, or serving in various volunteer positions. Include them and genuinely let them lead. Throughout this chapter, we will look at several important facets of leadership that apprentices must experience to become effective leaders one day.

YOUNG LEADERS MUST EXPERIENCE
THE DEMANDS OF LEADERSHIP

I have two "kids," and even though both are young adults, I still have an instinct to protect them. I don't want them to suffer any of life's hardships. But overprotecting isn't good for them. Life will present plenty of hardships, and learning how to deal with those challenges will help my children develop wisdom and character. This inner strength will enable them to handle the even tougher situations that will come their way. The same is true in ministry. I know it is common to want to protect those who serve under you, especially if they are young or inexperienced. But sheltering an apprentice from the uncomfortable aspects of leadership doesn't help him in the long run because he won't learn to lead.

> Sheltering your apprentices doesn't help them in the long run because they won't learn to lead.

It has been said that the church never sleeps, and those who lead it never sleep either. The latter part of that statement is an exaggeration, but most leaders understand the sentiment behind it. The ministry is relentless in both good and bad ways. It's good that leaders never give up their pursuit of the mission, but it's bad in that no matter how hard a pastor or ministry leader works, there is always more to do. The work is never done. In fact, when a pastor does a great job and his church grows, that actually creates more work! Apprentice leaders need to understand how to deal with that reality.

Exposing leaders in training to the demands of ministry does not mean dumping work on them. The right idea is to let them shoulder some of the pressure. Typically, a young or inexperienced leader will want to direct high-pressure situations to those in authority over them. Sometimes that's the right thing to do, and you need to be ready to help them. But most of the time, the young leaders need to solve the problem on their own, or at least do their best to solve it.

Recruiting volunteers is one of the most common pressures in the local church. No matter how big the congregation, the church always needs more people to serve on ministry teams. As the top leader, you may be tempted to jump in and save the day by doing all the recruiting. Perhaps you are faster and better at it than most of your leaders. Or maybe your leadership team has come to you in a panic, saying, "We need more volunteers—now!"

In both situations you have a choice. You can do it all on your own, or you can insist that your team join in solving the problem by doing some of the recruiting. This is a good opportunity to practice your equipping skills by teaching and showing your leaders how to invite someone onto a ministry team. You shouldn't abandon your leaders as they pursue new team members, but they will never reach their potential if you always bail them out.

Here's the tough question: When something isn't working, do you jump in and save the day, or let the person "crash and burn" so the apprentice leader can learn from the situation? The answer is, it depends. I know that's a frustrating answer, but it truly depends. It is overly simplistic to say apprentice leaders should be allowed to make as many mistakes as the ministry can sustain without subjecting itself to harm. The reality is, ministries can absorb some mistakes that won't ultimately harm them, and some of those errors may even cause the ministry to improve because it helps the leaders grow. If your leaders aren't making mistakes, they aren't leading.

However, apprentice leaders should not make the same mistake twice. This is an indication that the individual is not learning—and it is the secret to determining when you should jump in. Assuming you are coaching well, you should jump in if a leader begins to repeatedly make the same mistakes. At that point, you must protect that ministry area from the substantial negative impact of persistent errors that lead to eventual failure.

Young Leaders Must Experience the Service of Leadership

Leaders at the entry level of an organization aspire to be at the top one day. They believe that when they reach that place, they will be able to call the shots and do what they want. If you've been leading for any time at all, you're smiling with me because you know that belief couldn't be any more naive or untrue. The reality is that the less responsibility you have, the greater freedom you experience. The higher you climb in an organization, the more you must surrender your rights and privileges.

This is doubly true in the church. The casual church attender can do what he wants. He can complain, criticize, and even disrupt a worship service. He doesn't have to serve, give, or anything else. The opposite is true for leaders. They are called to serve and give up their rights and privileges for the sake of the ministry.

One of the best ways to test the servant quotient within leaders is to treat them like one. I don't mean you should treat them poorly. I mean you should assume that they are genuinely happy to serve. Treat each apprentice leader like nothing is too grand and nothing is too menial. I've met too many leaders who have an "I don't do windows" attitude, and they never do well leading people. They make it known that small tasks are beneath them. By behaving this way, they communicate that they are above others. No one wants to follow a leader like that.

Many years ago when John Maxwell was training me to teach the membership class at Skyline Wesleyan Church, I learned a powerful lesson by just watching him. John taught the class first, then he coached me on how to teach the next one. He watched me teach for about an hour, and I could tell he was taking some notes. Then he disappeared. I didn't understand what that meant and was a little nervous about it. John came back in about twenty minutes with coffee and doughnuts for everyone. He even poured coffee for each person.

What really struck me was that he was having a blast. He was thoroughly enjoying serving the people. He was the senior pastor, and I know he had other things to do. He didn't have to serve coffee, but there John was, just having the time of his life acting like he was a flight attendant aboard a Delta 767. Don't hesitate to give your leaders opportunities to pour coffee. If they can't serve with joy, they can't lead with integrity.

The serving leader embraces a life of giving more than receiving. A statement like that can easily sound like mere rhetoric or even propaganda, especially if it's not modeled. I hope serving is a natural, genuine, and foundational part of your lifestyle as a leader. If that is the case, it is likely that the apprentice leaders around you will "catch" that value from you and view it as a natural part of a leader's life. A spiritual leader who bases his or her behavior on the example of Jesus wakes up each day seeking ways to

> **Strong leaders embrace a life of giving more than receiving.**

153

strategically serve others. Leaders are not servants by accident. It's intentional.

Because leaders can't respond to everything, they must set priorities. This brings me to an important point. Leaders must be willing to say no. This is one of the toughest truths for a leader to learn. If you're a leader who loves people and wants to serve, I'm sure you have felt the tension of wanting to say yes to an opportunity to serve but not seeing how you could possibly add another item to your schedule. There are two things that have helped me find the right balance. First is knowing that my purpose is to build the church by serving people, not by making them happy. The second is realizing that my service must contribute to individuals' spiritual growth, not my comfort level. Weighing these two considerations has consistently helped me make the right choice.

Leaders who understand the importance of service will face another challenge. Because leaders operate in a giving mode most of the time, they must make time to refuel. This process is different for everyone, but the basics are similar. It may surprise you, but recharging your battery is not as much about being idle or literally doing nothing as it is about embracing a change of pace. Doing something out of the norm that you find enjoyable is often more energizing than just kicking back. Movies, for example, are great entertainment and a fun way to relax. But if you have only enough energy to watch a movie, you may be pushing too hard. Leaders serve because that is part of God's calling on their lives, but they can't forget to recharge or they will burn out and have nothing left to give.

YOUNG LEADERS MUST EXPERIENCE THE SACRIFICE OF LEADERSHIP

When apprentice leaders begin to embrace the leader's call to serve, they will soon experience the sacrifice of leadership. In a ministry setting, there is no growth without sacrifice. Jesus modeled this truth for us on the cross. You can serve when it's convenient, but you can't serve the way Jesus did without making sacrifices. We usually read Ephesians 5 in the context of a husband's leadership in the home. But let's read it again to see the picture it paints of Christ's sacrifice for the church.

> Husbands, love your wives, just as Christ loved the church and gave himself up for her to make her holy, cleansing her by the washing with water through the word, and to present her to himself as a radiant church, without stain or wrinkle or any other blemish, but holy and blameless. In this same way, husbands ought to love their wives as their own bodies. He who loves his wife loves himself. After all, no one ever hated his own body, but he feeds and cares for it, just as Christ does the church—for we are members of his body. "For this reason a man will leave his father and mother and be united to his wife, and the two will become one flesh." This is a profound mystery—but I am talking about Christ and the church. However, each one of you also must love his wife as he loves himself, and the wife must respect her husband.
>
> —EPHESIANS 5:25-33

Jesus gave up His life so the body of Christ could become what God intended—a radiant church without spot or wrinkle. No leader past, present, or future will ever make a sacrifice that compares to what Christ did for us, but we will often be called to put others above our own comfort and desires. For those in ministry leadership, sacrifice comes in a variety of forms, so let's look briefly at several of the more common sacrifices leaders must make.

Being carefree

It's easy for a leader to be in a sea of people and simultaneously experience the loneliness of leadership. No matter how much he might discuss an issue, or even come to a consensus with a board or leadership team, there comes a point at which the leader is responsible for the outcome of his decisions. We stand alone in that responsibility. Success or failure, in a sense, is on our shoulders. Whether you are the senior pastor, a small group leader, the head usher, or a support and recovery ministry leader, there are responsibilities you carry alone even though you don't do it all alone. That is leadership, and apprentice leaders must be aware of that reality.

Time

On many nights while my friends and family are relaxing in front of the TV or just chilling out, I am often busy finishing up some urgent item on my to-do list. This is a normal part of a leader's life. Of course, occasionally a great opportunity will force us to find more time. For me, this book is a good example of that. I invested more than two hundred hours writing and editing this project. Though this is an opportunity to fulfill a longtime goal of publishing this material, it's also strategic. It's part of my calling to invest in pastors and churches, and part of the purpose of 12Stone Church to invest in the next generation of leaders.

Leading people in ministry takes a tremendous amount of time. You can't rush a relationship, microwave a leader, or fast-track a process of life change. And when you tap into your purpose and passion, your list of things to do and the ministry opportunities that come your way will get longer, not shorter. Leadership costs you time. There is no way around it. The leaders you train must also understand this fact.

Finances

So what are you driving these days? A brand-new Ferrari or a Bentley? OK, how about a used Toyota? I really don't care what you drive, but I do care about the financial pressure you carry. It's difficult to lead well while under the weight of significant financial burdens. Let's be honest; many churches don't pay well, but there are also many leaders who don't manage their money well. It's complicated, I know. What is important is that we are generous and sacrificial in our financial giving. Many of the volunteer leaders you guide will be in a similar financial situation. They need you to model this kind of sacrifice well. They need you to understand the price tag of obedience and generosity, so you can show them the way.

These examples of sacrifice are not to be carried as a heavy burden. They are a privilege. Sacrifice keeps us in touch with God's love, patience, mercy, and humility. The call to sacrifice does not give leaders a license to punch the ever-handy martyr card many of us carry around. Your apprentice leaders should not think sacrifice is some kind of strange yet coveted ascetic lifestyle.

When their motives are right, sacrificial leaders are joyful leaders! Yet there is a balance to strike on this issue of sacrifice. I highly recommend that every leader make a short list of things he or she will not give up. Priorities such as your family, your health, and your walk with God should not be sidelined by ministry obligations. When you make that list, be sure to stick to it.

YOUNG LEADERS MUST EXPERIENCE THE PARTNERSHIP OF LEADERSHIP

Ministry is a partnership. Each time a new leader is added to the team, the group becomes larger, stronger, and capable of doing more. Apprentice leaders must know that great ministry doesn't happen in the midst of lone-ranger leadership. When a ministry's vision is clear and the team is united in pressing toward that goal, an unspoken partnership emerges among the leaders that bonds them together. I am privileged to experience this kind of partnership with 12Stone's staff, key volunteer leaders, and our senior pastor, Kevin Myers. Like all great partners, we know one another's strengths and weakness. We lean into those strengths and help cover the areas where one partner is weaker.

For example, Kevin is strong in helping people experience spiritual breakthrough while I am strong in developing processes for building leaders and making our ministry systems more efficient. This doesn't mean God can't use me to help someone experience a breakthrough or that Kevin can't develop a systemic process. This means we each apply our knowledge and energy toward the areas we are strongest in.

Kevin regularly sits down with people and skillfully engages them in conversations that deliver the impact of a spiritual knockout punch. They discover brilliant insights, and the person is usually inspired to make significant life changes. But they don't always know what to do next or how to do it. That's where I step in. My part often requires a series of lengthy conversations to help someone understand and live out the new breakthrough.

Great partnerships have a way of purifying leaders' motives. To make a partnership work, leaders must set their agendas aside (not the vision, but any personal agendas). Wise leaders remain open to new ways of doing things and are gracious enough to accept that things will not always go their way. This is what you have to give up to go up. If you let other strong leaders on the team, they will have differing opinions. And if they are putting great ideas on the table, you would be wise to consider them. You won't always get the credit or public attention when you participate in a partnership. But receiving credit should not be your goal. In fact, I hope your ministry develops such a strong culture of giving credit away that it becomes second nature for your team members to celebrate other leaders' contributions over their own.

When I think of great partnerships, John Lennon and Paul McCartney of The Beatles are among those at the top of my list. They formed one of the most brilliant songwriting partnerships in the early history of rock 'n' roll music. They wrote hundreds of songs together, many of which became No. 1 hits and are still popular to this day, more than forty years later. As a fan, I've enjoyed watching clips and interviews over the years, and it seems to me that it wasn't just the applause of the crowd that spurred them on to do better and better work. It was the power of their partnership that pushed them to keep reaching for new heights as songwriters. I think they knew they were better together than apart.

A similar process is at work in the church. When leaders dream and pray together, it sharpens the ministry's focus and sense of purpose. I'm part of the elder board at 12Stone, and when we all talk and pray together, God grants us His favor and kindness. It matters who prays. I don't believe any one person's prayers are more important to God, but it is important that the leaders pray. And praying *together* is an especially big deal. Prayer knits hearts together and solidifies unity on the team. When prayer is a central feature in the partnership, conflict is minimized and differences are downplayed.

Partnership satisfies the heart of God. Covenant is a dominant theme throughout the Bible, and it is largely relational in nature. The covenant points to God's redemptive relationship with man. When leaders are in a right covenant relationship, God is pleased. When the family of God operates within the covenant framework of love and unity, and the kingdom advances as a result, it warms God's heart.

Partnerships between spiritual leaders fit the same pattern. God designed us to work together, not independently. There is a need for strong, visionary leaders, but they must work with others or the vision will not become a reality. From Moses and Joshua to Paul and Timothy, there are many great partnerships in the Bible. Each has a story to tell about how the partners made each other better. This is central to what you and I want to pass on to the next generation of leaders in the church.

Young Leaders Must Experience the Rewards of Leadership

As we expose apprentice leaders to the more challenging aspects of leadership—the service, sacrifices, and demands of ministry— we must remember to include them in the times of celebration. The road a leader travels can get long and weary. In ministry, we don't view leadership as a burden, but it is good to be honest about its difficulties. Most leaders readily shoulder the tough parts of their role, and if you've been following my recommendations in this chapter, you will have allowed your apprentice leaders to experience these less glamorous aspects as well. But it's important that neither you nor your apprentice miss the moments that call for a celebration.

It's interesting that in general, most leaders either over-celebrate or under-celebrate. Leaders who have found a good balance are somewhat rare. I certainly haven't perfected this. I lean toward under-celebrating. I'm a driven, type A personality. As soon as I accomplish something, I'm ready to move on to the next initiative. This is true for me and leaders like me because we naturally think ahead and strive for progress. As I've matured (OK, as I've gotten older), I've become much better about stopping to smell the roses and celebrate with the team.

This isn't a problem for the smaller group of leaders who "over-celebrate." These folks know how to have fun. I met a pastor once who said to me, "I never let work get in the way of a good party!" He was an entertaining guy, but the downside was that he didn't get much done. None of us should live remotely close to either extreme. It's up to each of us to discover the right balance for ourselves, our churches, and the leaders we serve with.

There are three ways to think about celebrating the victories as you include leaders in the rewards of leadership. First is the way you reflect upon the reward internally. The reward of leadership is knowing you walk with integrity and live to please the Father. There is no greater reward than hearing God consistently say to you, "Well done." The apostle Paul often commented on this. He wrote in Galatians 1:10, "Am I now trying to win the approval of men, or of God? Or am I trying to please men? If I were still trying to please men, I would not be a servant of Christ." Your quiet and inner reflection on these things will become part of your leadership DNA and will impact those you include in leadership with you.

Second is the way you recognize and experience the rewards of ministry externally with other leaders. It is unlikely that the leaders you include, develop, and empower will see their rewards as something material that they are owed. I hope that would not be the case for volunteer leaders either, and most staff members don't seek a material reward for their ministry service.

Any spiritual leader who wants to be rewarded for their service with material things will be consistently frustrated and disappointed. Material rewards are not inappropriate, but they should not be a leader's motivation. External rewards come in a number of forms, from public recognition to expressions of gratitude such as a celebratory lunch or a dinner out. The richness of these rewards is deep and lasting when they are received without having been sought. Servant leaders keep the real meaning of rewards in perspective.

The third way to think about how you enjoy the rewards of ministry is to consider the way you celebrate corporately. The Old and New Testaments have many examples of feasts, banquets, and parties to celebrate the faithfulness of God and His enduring love, provision, and protection. It is equally fitting for you to celebrate the goodness of God in your ministry. As you experience moments of victory and success, enjoy the moment with your entire fellowship.

In December 2010 we literally toasted a moment of victory during our worship services at 12Stone. We received a miraculous offering that enabled us to feed more than five thousand unemployed families in our county. This meant the families received a Christmas dinner and a week's worth of groceries. We celebrated with individual bottles of sparkling cider—one for everyone. At the end of the sermon we lifted the bottles along with our praise to God and quoted Psalm 117—"Praise the Lord, all you nations... for great is his love toward us, and the faithfulness of the Lord endures forever."

It was a great moment that marked a miracle of God. Choose

ways that make sense in your culture and environment, but don't miss out on having some fun as a congregation. God is pleased when we experience the rewards of leadership and invite our apprentices to join us. God receives the glory, and He blesses us and the ministries we lead.

As you can see from the image below, we have almost completed the leadership development process. We began the journey by establishing a relationship, and the powerful conclusion is launching a new leader! The fifth and final part of the process is just a page away. In this last section we will look at two powerful skills for mentoring new leaders—the ability to *develop* and the ability to *empower*.

AMPLIFY YOUR LEADERSHIP

Establish a Relationship	→	Engage a Follower	→	Embrace a Team Member	→	Coach an Apprentice	→	Mentor a New Leader
• *Connect* at the heart • *Appreciate* people for who they are		• *Encourage* people to bring out their best • *Inspire* people to follow the vision		• *Invite* individuals into meaningful ministry • *Equip* team members for ministry success		• *Select* the best potential leaders • *Include* emerging leaders to give them relevant experience		

PART
FIVE

MENTOR A NEW LEADER

Each new leader who emerges is a great gift to the kingdom of God.

'LL NEVER FORGET the day I received my first guitar. It was Christmas Day, and I was twelve years old. I was so excited I couldn't sleep that Christmas Eve. When Christmas morning arrived, there it was—the exact guitar I had circled in the catalog. It was a Sears Silvertone solid body with a look similar to a Fender Jaguar. (Don't laugh, but I would love to have a late-sixties Silvertone like that now.) My parents bought me the Silvertone amp too. I was ready to be a rock star! There was only one problem. I couldn't play guitar.

I needed someone to teach me, and my neighbor Mario was just the person I needed. He was probably only about sixteen years old, but to a skinny, quiet twelve-year-old like me, he was the coolest. Mario not only played an electric guitar, he also was athletic and had that inexplicable charisma that made everyone want to be around him.

Why he let me in, I'll never know, but I'm grateful he chose to teach me how to play the guitar. I wasn't bothered by my lack of natural talent because Mario said I would be able to play well if I practiced hard every day. That made a profound impact on me. To this day I understand the value of dreams and desires and how they are connected to hard work. I never became a rock star, but there is no question that Mario's encouragement greatly affected my confidence in life.

When I was twelve, I needed someone to show me how to play the guitar. When I graduated from seminary, I needed someone to show me how to lead in ministry. In both cases I needed a mentor. Several leaders have coached me, including my primary mentor John Maxwell. I admit that I have been very fortunate. That's part of my motivation to write this book. Because John and others mentored me in leadership, I'm passionate about mentoring others.

That's what good leaders do. They teach others how to lead. It doesn't matter if you mentor ten leaders or hundreds in your lifetime. What matters is that you mentor someone. Are you investing in any new leaders? If so, how are you making a difference in their lives? Will someone lead better because of you?

Most leaders are tempted to lead everything themselves. But I trust that if you've read this far, you are enthusiastic about raising up new leaders. This will dramatically increase your ministry's ability to reach more people for Jesus and see lives changed for the good.

Mentoring is where the rubber meets the road. The previous

eight skills we've looked at are critical, but this is where apprentices begin to transform into new leaders. Look back at what we've covered so far. We begin the process by connecting with and demonstrating genuine appreciation for new friends or new relationships in general. Soon we engage them as followers through encouragement and inspiration. From among the followers, we begin to embrace new team members by inviting them to serve with us and equipping them for successful ministry. Then from those ministry teams we select individuals with leadership potential and begin to include them in the responsibilities of leadership.

Coaching these fresh apprentices is fun. And in Part Five you will see these emerging leaders launched into action as you develop and empower them. As I mentioned before, developmental time lines are fluid, and there is overlap in the mentoring process. Rarely will you use each skill in perfect sequence, but you do need to use them all. One of the primary reasons many leaders are not ready to lead, and don't lead well, is that their leadership development process was short-circuited at some point.

Again, there is a "blend and blur" quality to the process. And it's OK to adjust your strategy after you have proven that you understand and consistently practice all the skills needed to cultivate new leaders. When this leadership development process becomes second nature, you can put your own spin on it. It's like learning to ski or play tennis. You must master the fundamentals before you attempt to improvise. When you improvise before you have gained adequate experience, you will cheat your apprentice leaders, which will ultimately hurt your ministry.

No matter how much raw talent a leader may have, he or she needs mentoring. Even when you hire new staff, don't assume they have mastered a particular level of leadership. Earning an academic degree and receiving a paycheck for leading in ministry don't make a person fully ready to lead. Mentoring is continual. The demand gets lighter as leaders grow in their ability, but the need for mentoring never ends.

What will make you a good mentor? I could draft a long list of attributes of good mentors, but I want to focus in on three that cover the most fundamental requirements.

Demonstrating a willingness to be with them.

It is possible to impress people from a distance, but you can impact them only by being near them. Jesus modeled this principle with the leaders He chose to mentor. We read in Mark 3 that He intentionally drew His disciples close.

> Jesus went up on a mountainside and called to him those he wanted, and they came to him. He appointed twelve—designating them apostles—that they might be *with* him and that he might send them out to preach.
> —MARK 3:13-14, EMPHASIS ADDED

When it comes to leadership development, much of it must come from another leader who gets in the trenches to show the way. Mentoring is not all done up close because leaders can learn a lot from books, conferences, CDs, and so on. There is also great benefit in leveraging technology, which today can range from simple conference calls to sophisticated webinars. But without a mentor or two within physical proximity, the aspiring leader will not get the most out of the development process.

In the early years of my leadership development, John was always nearby. In fact, I knew where he would be nearly every afternoon. John spent an hour or so completing administrative tasks in his little office down the hall from mine. This was different from the time he spent in his "upper room" study. When John was in his office, I would drop in and tell him what I was working on and fire off a few questions. In these few minutes we would have great coaching conversations.

One of the unique aspects of our interaction was that I never sat down. I never presumed upon his time and would always try to "read him" to discern whether or not he truly had the time, because I knew he would give me his attention even if he was busy. Please understand, mentoring isn't time to "hang out." The process is enjoyable, and deep friendships can emerge, but it is first and foremost a purposeful endeavor. Its primary goal is to prepare a new leader.

Relentlessly asking questions and challenging aspiring leaders

This is one of my strengths as a developer of leaders. In fact, my family says I can drive a normal person crazy with my tendency to ask an "unending" stream of questions. So I guess I should stay focused on leaders and avoid the normal people. (I'm joking.) What can I say; I come by it honestly. My first job out of college was as a private investigator. That certainly didn't help. Or maybe it did.

Some leaders say the secret to asking good questions is to always know the next question you will ask. I disagree. If you always know the next question you will ask, you may be a great debater but not likely an effective mentor. Your next question needs to incorporate what you learned from the previous answer. Great questions come from discerning listening and not from a canned mental script.

You should have a direction in mind, but the complete journey shouldn't be mapped out. The better you get at asking the right questions, the more effective you will become at challenging the right leaders on the right issues at the right times.

Interpreting and translating leadership techniques in a way the new leader can understand

One of the most dangerous things an inexperienced leader can do is tell the person he is mentoring what he knows! I realize that may sound confusing, but allow me to explain. If an inexperienced leader is, for example, a hammer, everything will appear to be a nail. If the leader is a bandage, everything will appear to be a cut or scrape. Leaders who have only one game play or solution for every situation don't make effective mentors. Every person is different and requires a different approach.

As a mentor you are responsible to understand the new leader's frame of reference, determine what he knows, and assess what he can do. If you can't interpret what he knows, you won't be able to translate your leadership lessons well. The aspiring leader will not understand what you're saying and will therefore be unlikely to satisfy what you're asking of him. It helps that you are there to show the person. He can watch you, and in turn you can coach him as he performs specific tasks. But you still must be able to see the situation through that individual's eyes.

This requires spending time with the person you are mentoring and asking great questions! There are times when you'll say to a new leader, "This is how you do it." Or, "This is the answer." Or even simply, "No." But the best mentoring leads a person to discover answers for himself. Remember, leadership development is not something you can do for someone. The primary responsibility for learning and growing resides within the emerging leader himself. Your job is to mentor!

Chapter Nine

DEVELOP NEW LEADERS

The development process transforms lives.

Paul Piraino is the executive pastor at Victory Highway Wesleyan Church in Painted Post, New York. He joined their team in 1989 as the pastor of student ministries. One of the intriguing things about his ministry journey is that since he arrived, the church has had four senior pastors. Paul just keeps running them off!

In all seriousness, one of the most powerful things Paul said to me was that after so many years in one church, he'd do it all over again. I asked him why, and Paul said each senior pastor had contributed to his life and developed him as a leader in different ways.

When leaders stay, that is nearly always the reason. They are being developed.

Jerry Jack was the senior pastor when Paul arrived. Under Jerry's leadership, Paul said he found great clarity in his call to ministry. In fact, if Jerry had not helped Paul find greater confidence in his call, Paul might not have remained in ministry. It was during those early years that Paul also was encouraged to develop the relational side of his ministry.

Even after so many years, Paul speaks of each of the four senior pastors fondly. Paul said under the next senior pastor, Larry Eastlack, he discovered a more assertive side of his personality developed. He learned to speak up when problems arose, and he became solution-oriented.

David LeRoy was the third pastor. Under David's leadership, Paul said he developed a greater sense of confidence in himself as a leader. Paul said David truly believed in him, and that was life changing. Paul told me there were times when David believed things about him before he believed them about himself.

Today the senior pastor is Steve McEuen. Under Steve's leadership Paul has discovered and developed a more intuitive side of his leadership. He has become more spontaneous as a leader and communicator. Paul says his skills and leadership capacity have deepened through Steve's gracious transfer of significant authority and trust.

In the years Paul has served at Victory Wesleyan, he has seen the church's average attendance grow from three hundred to nearly fifteen hundred. That is significant, particularly in a town with a population of nine thousand. The nearest sister town, Corning, New York, has a population of nineteen thousand. Paul is a good leader who has poured his heart into Victory. And his leadership has made a huge difference at the church. Paul, his wife, Christine, and their three daughters are blessed to have received this investment through the years. Now it is Paul's passion and privilege to develop the leaders around him.

Principles for Developing New Leaders

The pastors and ministry leaders at 12Stone consistently say the same two things attract them to join the team. The first is our "wild-eyed, no-plan-B vision." And the second is our promise to develop them as leaders. These two qualities are embedded in the life and ministry of the church through the staff, and they continue to draw new leaders to the team. Like Paul, we all want to have someone invest in us, and in turn we develop others. That is what this chapter is all about. Developing leaders is a skill that can be improved if you keep a few principles in mind.

Don't stop growing.

Years ago when we lived in San Diego, Patti and I took a romantic hot air balloon ride. It was just the two of us and the captain in a beautifully colored balloon. When we were ready to start our ascent, the captain fired off the burners, and, boy, were they loud. I knew the captain would have to fire the burners to fill the balloon with hot air so it would rise and we could enjoy a great flight. What I didn't realize was that he would continue to fire off the burners in a consistent and strategic manner throughout the flight.

I thought that after the air was heated, it would somehow magically stay trapped in the balloon. I admit, I was more interested in Patti and our romantic picnic than the physics of the flight. But I was too curious about the burners to leave it alone. When I asked the captain why he kept lighting the burners, the expression on his face was a cross between "I need to be nice because you paid a lot of money" and "Are you really that stupid?" He smiled and said, "If I don't continually heat the air, we're going down!"

Leaders who are good at developing others make an intentional effort to keep improving personally. They keep the fire inside hot. You may have years of experience and be well beyond the level of the person you are mentoring, but eventually you will have little to offer if you stop growing as a leader. If you don't keep the fires hot, your "leadership balloon" is going to come down!

Do you reinvent yourself? This is not about changing your basic personality, keeping up with the latest trends, or whether you should tuck in your shirt. (That's one of the top three spiritual tensions I deal with—to tuck or not to tuck!) Reinventing yourself is about staying out of a comfort zone. Any leader can fall into this place of comfort if he is not growing, stretching, learning, and changing. It is lethal to a leader when everything is balanced, stable, known, and in pleasant symmetry.

> **Leaders who are good at developing others make an intentional effort to keep improving personally.**

If this is happening to you, it's time to shake things up. You may ultimately make adjustments in your church or ministry, but the kind of shaking I'm talking about takes place in you. It's important for you as a leader to push yourself to a new level of leadership. And if you're really moving toward growth, the process will be uncomfortable. You may even want to give up. You won't naturally want to make the needed changes, which is why the growth process I'm talking about requires discipline.

It's like working out. When I'm on the exercise bike, I can easily ride at a level seven for forty-five minutes. But if I wanted to ride at a level ten for forty-five minutes, I would have to reinvent myself physically to maintain that pace for that period of time. This is a simple example, but it illustrates the point. Growth requires change, and that can be uncomfortable, but all leaders must continually stretch themselves. No matter how many people they lead or what status they achieve in ministry, all leaders must keep pressing to reach new levels.

How are you doing in this area? Are you pushing yourself in ways that utilize your gifts but challenge you to dig in and discover new territory intellectually, emotionally, or spiritually? Whatever that new territory is for you, it won't simply be a matter of working harder to do more of the same. Instead, you may have to work smarter and create more margin in your life so you can find the time to develop yourself as a leader. This is how you keep your spiritual fire hot. This is how you continue building yourself from within. If you don't fill yourself up with fresh knowledge about leadership, insights into ministry, and revelation from the Holy Spirit, you will have little to give out to those you mentor.

Focus on relationships and results.

If there's one thing I love, it's hanging out with pastors and volunteer church leaders, drinking tea at Starbucks and talking church. But this is where one of my strengths can become a weakness if I don't pay attention. I so enjoy hearing people's stories and talking about ministry that I sometimes miss opportunities to press in to see how that leader needs to grow. Relationships are great, and they mean the world to me, but results matter too. The best leaders want me to not only listen to them but also challenge them on their personal growth.

I admit that I have a bias for relationship and a desire to encourage others. Sometimes that alone is valuable. Connecting on a personal level is part of the developing process for both apprentice leaders and those who have been in the trenches for decades. But relationship cannot take precedence over a leader's personal progress. This is because there is a direct relationship between the growth of the leader and the growth of the church. That fact is simply irrefutable.

Learning to combine relationship and results is one of the secrets to great mentoring. A good relationship cultivates trust and makes the developing process enjoyable. Who wouldn't want that? Yet here's where it gets tricky. A mentoring relationship that is all business usually doesn't last long. However, when a relationship gets very comfortable, particularly when it has lasted for a long period of time, the expectations for growth can slowly diminish. There is a balance to strike.

John Maxwell has modeled this so well for me. He has a unique ability to mix work and play. We might talk about a book project while at a baseball game, or we may take a night to enjoy a great meal with friends while on a foreign mission trip. One of the best phrases I learned from John was, "Always bring something to the table." What that means is no matter what the situation—work or play, serious or light—always add value. That doesn't have to be complicated or boring. The value could be telling a great story that entertains everyone. It might be sharing a new idea or something you learned from an interesting person you just met.

John continues to model this today. While in Florida recently, Patti and I went to dinner with John and his wife, Margaret, and another friend of ours. The meeting was spontaneous, and we were just out to enjoy some time together. But before long John was telling us about a great book he was reading on leadership. I couldn't write down the title fast enough. And I know the next time John sees me, he will no doubt ask me what I learned from the book.

When you mentor someone, enjoy the relationship but be serious about seeing results. I know two leaders whom I'll call Eric and Tony. Eric is pastor of a smaller church that can't afford a paid worship leader. Tony is a gifted singer and musician who is young and inexperienced in leadership. Tony led worship at Eric's church, but mostly by himself because he wasn't good at gathering and leading a worship team.

Eric coached him for months but didn't see any results, so he gave Tony an ultimatum. He had to step up as a leader even though he was a volunteer, or he would be relieved of his position as worship leader. This was a difficult line in the sand for Eric to draw because the two enjoyed a great personal relationship. But Eric's determination to see his friend grow paid off.

It turned out that Tony never took leadership seriously because he didn't view himself as a leader, just as a volunteer musician. When he began to see himself differently, little by little he started to develop a solid worship team, and he ultimately became a good leader. Eric loved Tony, but he was willing to make a significant change in Tony's role in the church if there were no results. This is what a good mentoring relationship requires—commitment to both friendship and development.

Don't try to make someone different.

As a mentor, you can help build a person up, but you can't make him into someone different. When you attempt to do that, you rob that individual of the opportunity to maximize his potential as a leader. I often tell the pastors I coach that when we develop a leader, we make him bigger, better, and stronger. But we don't make him into someone new. A wise leader does not try to give a person qualities he doesn't naturally possess but works with the design God has placed within that individual.

A person's basic wiring—his temperament, energy level, pace, and biases—are fixed for the most part. That's one of the reasons the selection process is so important. You can help leaders improve their attitude, understanding, skills, and even personal vision, but it's vital that you let them be who they are. Part of this reflects on you as the mentor, so let me ask you a personal question. Do you like who you are? Developing people is far more art than science, and those you mentor will pick up on what is going on inside you. You can teach leadership skills in a somewhat emotionally detached manner, but significant impact comes only when you connect at a heart level.

When you like who you are and are comfortable with yourself, that will come through and greatly enhance the mentoring process. If you struggle with who you are, the people you develop will likely perceive a sense of distance. This will keep them from fully trusting you, and they won't want to follow your leadership. If you're uncomfortable in your own skin, it will be beneficial for you to strengthen your self-image through wise counsel. When you like yourself, you don't waste emotional energy trying to be someone else. You have margin to invest time and energy in others, which is essential for developing leaders. What's more, when you like who you are, you are much more likely to give the person you're mentoring the latitude to be himself also.

A friend of mine whom I'll call Sheryl was mentoring a young leader named Judy in basic human nature and people skills. Judy wasn't good with administrative details, but Sheryl hadn't paid much attention to that because they weren't focusing on those skills. But Judy's boss at the church was becoming frustrated with her inability to perform administrative tasks, so Sheryl asked me for ways to coach Judy in this area. Detail is not my great strength either, but I knew I could offer ideas that would help Judy get more organized and, perhaps, use her time more wisely.

After meeting with Sheryl a couple more times, Judy set some new practices in place, and she made noticeable improvement. Yet Sheryl called me a few months later and said that though Judy had improved in her organizational ability, her boss was still upset. At this point I began to connect the dots. I realized Judy's boss didn't want her to improve her organizational skills; he wanted her to become a different person.

I told Sheryl that Judy would never be a super-organized, detail maniac. That is simply not who she is. We talked at length about how important it is to develop someone to be better, not different. Then after some long conversations, we all agreed that because a certain level of organizational prowess is required to keep any professional job or volunteer leadership role, Judy would need to find a way to cover her details. Because the church could not afford to give Judy a paid assistant, she would have to find a volunteer assistant.

Judy invited a great volunteer in the church to help her eight hours a week. That worked out so well that she recruited another assistant and ended up with sixteen hours of volunteer administrative help. Each person came in two days a week for four hours a day. It worked out great for everyone. With Sheryl's help, Judy developed into a better leader while staying true to herself.

Putting the Process Into Practice

With these principles in mind, it is time to put the development process into practice. The following strategies are not difficult to implement, but they will profoundly impact the effectiveness of your mentoring program. Mentoring requires a significant time investment, and these practices will help you make the most of it.

1. Establish a simple plan.

During a sermon once at North Point Community Church, Andy Stanley painted a picture of his vision for his family in one sentence. He said something along the lines of, "Sandra and I want to create an environment that our kids want to come back to after they are grown and out on their own." What a simple yet profound thought. With it Andy set a goal he and his wife will be working toward for decades.

Do you have a vision for new leaders? Can you paint a clear picture of it? The list of qualities included in my vision for new leaders isn't long. I want to develop a person of influence who demonstrates a strategic, servant lifestyle to advance God's kingdom. Knowing your vision creates a map for your mentoring process that will guide you step by step for the long haul.

Each leader will have a different plan, but write it down. Keep it short and simple. If you include too many steps, you are almost guaranteed not to stick with it. And I promise you, a long list will change before you get through it. Less is more. Keep the big picture in mind as you mentor, but work on one item at a time.

I once mentored a young student leader who was a gifted but undisciplined communicator. Doug's teaching gift was so strong he could communicate with little to no preparation. But when Doug and I met, his tendency to under-prepare was beginning to catch up with him. It was easy to see that in time it would absolutely prevent him from becoming the leader he could be.

Cheating your gift cheats your church or the ministry organization you serve, and that just doesn't make sense. For Doug, I created a one-point development plan. I required one simple thing of him. He had to turn in his teaching notes for review every week by Thursday. His supervisor and I reviewed the notes, and we used them to coach Doug. We weren't really interested in Doug's notes. We wanted to challenge him to develop a simple discipline. Although Doug was already a good communicator, he became noticeably better. And when he saw how the discipline of preparation improved an area he was already gifted in, Doug began to transfer what he had learned to other areas of his leadership that needed improvement.

As you use your plan to help people develop specific skills, remember to nurture the people you're mentoring. This entire process begins with establishing a relationship, which requires connection and appreciation. These are to be followed by encouragement. All of these skills remain vital throughout the leadership development process. How you incorporate them will shift according to the length, depth, and maturity of the relationship, but they will continue to be necessary.

Believe me, at times the areas you focus on for development will not be fun for you or the person you're mentoring to address. The level of nurturing you have invested in the relationship will make all the difference. Instead of resisting you, the person will stick with you for as long as it takes if they know you care.

A friend of mine was mentoring his head usher, whom I'll call Ronnie. My friend led a mid-size church that had two Sunday services. The ushers team included about thirty men and women, and each service required about eight ushers; therefore sixteen ushers were needed each weekend. Ronnie rotated the ushers so they didn't need to serve every Sunday. But despite his ability to organize his team and develop good guidelines for them, he had a major flaw. He lacked people skills.

He desperately needed to incorporate a spirit of grace and kindness. In fact, the situation became so bad that Ronnie's supervisor gave him an ultimatum. If Ronnie didn't improve, he would no longer be the head usher. You've heard the saying before, but it is so true: people don't care how much you know until they know how much you care. After six months of tough conversations, Ronnie made it to the next level. And he will tell you that one reason he stuck in there was because he knew his leaders challenged him because they cared about him and saw his potential to become an even better leader.

> **Knowing your productive strengths and destructive weaknesses will give you greater focus and cause you to make a stronger impact.**

2. Focus on productive strengths.

It is helpful to know your strengths and weaknesses, but it is even better to understand your *productive* strengths and *destructive* weaknesses. Knowing this will give you greater focus and cause you to make a stronger impact. The same is true with those you mentor. It is largely a waste of time to pour effort and energy into developing a person's weaknesses. Making slight improvements in an area the person is not gifted in doesn't add much value to his or her overall leadership. When I coach and mentor leaders, the only weaknesses I pay much attention to are the ones that harm their relationships with God or others. That is where the rubber meets the road for anyone in ministry.

If a leader is struggling with relationships in general, it's necessary to invest all the time needed to turn that around. The same is true concerning a leader's relationship with God. If a spiritual leader is not walking closely with God, he won't be able to do much that will have a lasting impact. I find it interesting that in both our relationships with God and with people, communication is a foundational element. Typically, leaders who struggle with relationships need to take time to listen and respond to the other person's needs. When they do this, it's amazing how much better their relationships become. Similarly, listening and responding through prayer will deepen a leader's connection to God in profound ways. In fact, there is no limit to the level of intimacy a person can enjoy through meaningful conversation.

With a solid relational foundation to build upon, you can focus your mentoring on developing the areas of a leader's life that will have the strongest impact. If you think about it, what is more likely to bring a leader through a rough patch when he is struggling, his strengths or weaknesses? Of course, the answer is his strengths—and more specifically his productive strengths. We all have strengths that are useful but not consistently productive. For instance, I can play the guitar. I love music, and I hear more than the average nonmusician. But I'm still not a musician. I would be completely and utterly lost if I attempted to play on the platform with our worship team. Although it enhances my life in general, my musical ability is not a productive strength. No matter how many lessons I take from the greatest of teachers, I will never be a good guitar player. If I made that a goal, I would fail.

I often see leaders fall prey to developing their strengths of interest rather than their productive strengths. One of the most common examples I've seen through the years is of leaders who want to teach. These leaders are godly people who definitely have an ability to teach, but that is not a productive strength for them. No matter how hard they work at it, they don't see the same level of fruit (life change) from teaching that they would see from other areas they are gifted in.

There are two words I often use to encourage senior pastors whose dominant gift is not communication but who want to develop their teaching ability: preach shorter. And sometimes I coach them to consider inviting a pastor on staff to teach several times a year alongside them. Then I coach them to devote their time to leveraging their more dominant gifts and strengths. One pastor I coached was an average teacher, but he was brilliant in strategic leadership. I encouraged him to develop his leadership gift, and the results were clearly evident. Instead of being discouraged that he didn't become a better teacher, he's happier now that he is an even more brilliant strategic leader!

When it comes to volunteer leaders, I take a slightly different tact. I nearly always coach them to use their desire to teach by leading a small group. This allows them to teach, but it is not the primary emphasis of their leadership. Their goal is to focus on discussion, interaction, and ultimately the same result all ministry leaders are after—life change.

Helping a leader discover and leverage his productive strengths is one of your primary responsibilities as a mentor. This will take effort and energy, but it is an essential part of your role. And the results make it so worth it. Of course, leaders cannot do only what they want to do. This is not what it means to leverage one's productive strengths. Every leader must fulfill certain basic leadership responsibilities before he will gain the freedom to leverage his most productive strengths.

3. Insist on progress.

A good mentor requires improvement in the life and leadership of the one being mentored. Mentoring new leaders is not an altruistic process. You may be selfless and giving as a mentor, and that is good, but the leadership development process requires a productive outcome. When you invest your time mentoring someone, it is not acceptable for that person to waste the gift you are giving. You have a limited amount of time, and it is precious. You can't afford to invest months or years in someone who is not making progress.

It is a sad reality, but not every mentoring relationship goes well. The chemistry may be off, or the person may not have his heart in it. Perhaps the timing isn't right. There are many possible reasons. On more than one occasion I have told someone I was mentoring, "I need to see that you are working for you as hard as I am!" But I don't end a mentoring relationship quickly or easily. In fact, if a leader is struggling, I usually become his chief cheerleader until he regains momentum.

But when someone consistently doesn't prepare, doesn't get things done, and doesn't try, I strongly recommend that you have a candid conversation and set a time limit for him or her to get back in the game. This breakdown in the mentoring process is rarely because of the person's competence and nearly always because of his attitude. If the person doesn't change his attitude and continues to fail to get things done, you would be wise to end the mentoring relationship. This doesn't mean you stop caring about the person or that you no longer have any relationship with him. It means you stop investing time in mentoring that individual.

Progress requires truth. Too often a local church leader will say it's OK for a new leader to slack off on his end of the mentoring partnership. It's not. The kingdom of God is not to be taken lightly. While I hope you and I do not take ourselves too seriously, we need to take the mission seriously. So let me be blunt. Leaders must step up or step out. Years ago I saw a bumper sticker that said, "Lead, follow, or get out of the way." That slogan isn't warm and fuzzy, but it tells the truth.

Leaders must face the truth. And the truth is, some leaders are lazy. Yes, we want to extend grace to them, but that doesn't mean we ignore their behavior. Sometimes extending grace means having a tough conversation. The apostle Paul said it well in Ephesians 4.

> Instead, speaking the truth in love, we will in all things grow up into him who is the Head, that is, Christ. From him the whole body, joined and held together by every supporting ligament, grows and builds itself up in love, as each part does its work.
>
> —EPHESIANS 4:15-16

These two verses instruct us not only to speak the truth in love but also to do our part to build the kingdom. The up-and-coming leaders are counting on you to speak truth into their lives, even when it's uncomfortable.

The goal of developing leaders is to bring out the best in each person. This is what you do as a mentor—you bring out the best! And no matter how much you may want quick results, mentoring is a process, not a program or an event. You can't just add water, stir, and produce an excellent leader. Developing people is not a microwaveable project. It is a long and slow simmer of strategic intentionality. As a mentor, you are helping leaders acquire skills that will benefit them in all aspects of their life. When you invest in developing a person, you improve the whole person and help him reach a higher level.

From helping the person cultivate certain disciplines to inspiring him to have a positive attitude, you are changing a life! Use mistakes as tools for growth and always believe the best. This process is personal. The principles don't change, but every leader you mentor will be different. Each one will require you to understand how he is wired, how he communicates, when to push him, and when to nurture and encourage him. In the end there's nothing quite like mentoring. I consider it an honor and a privilege to invest in future leaders.

Chapter Ten

EMPOWER EFFECTIVE LEADERS TO REALIZE THEIR POTENTIAL

Transferring authority releases new leaders to fulfill their potential and advance the mission of the church.

THERE IS A currency through which leaders get things done. It's called authority. Some people prefer to use the term influence, and that word does more accurately describe the innate function of leadership. But, ultimately, if a leader can't handle authority, he or she can't lead.

Leaders often struggle with authority. Some take advantage of it, and others barely act on it. Some overstep their authority, and others hide behind it. Yet the wisest of leaders understands that authority doesn't really belong to them. They are given the responsibility to steward it with wisdom, grace, and strength of character. But they are not its source. This is a truth anyone who is serious about empowering new leaders must wholeheartedly embrace. The implication is that the ministry does not belong to you. The complication is that you are still held responsible.

All authority is transferred.

There are two primary sources of authority: God and man. In ministry, the two are intricately connected. Ultimately, God is the source of a spiritual leader's authority, but if our understanding of authority stops there, we could easily become answerable to no one. A classic example is when a church board says to the pastor, "We were here long before you, and we'll be here long after you're gone." With that statement, the board is communicating that they own and run the church, and report to no one. Scary!

A pastor can do something similar by overleveraging and therefore misusing his leadership. When a minister abandons a healthy fear of his sacred vocation and begins to brazenly declare that he owns the ministry, he has misappropriated authority. When a volunteer leader changes her thinking from "our" ministry to "my" ministry, she is misappropriating authority. This is not what God had in mind. Benevolent dictators eventually lead poorly because they can't see past themselves.

All authority is transferred. I have a tremendous amount of authority at 12Stone Church, but it is not *my* authority. It has been transferred to me by the senior pastor, Kevin Myers. I merely steward that authority. The Directional Leadership Team (DLT) and our campus pastors also have significant leadership authority, but it does not belong to them either. It also has been transferred to them to steward for the good of others.

Let's look at this from another angle. Kevin Myers carries huge authority as the senior pastor of 12Stone, but it is granted and sustained by the local church board, which answers to the officials of the Wesleyan Church. The simple principle here is that all ministry authority has been transferred, and therefore we must hold it loosely as we lead others, remembering we are stewards and not owners. It's amazing how relaxed everyone could be if this were genuinely embraced.

Jesus never spoke of His authority apart from its connection to the Father. Jesus received His authority from the Father and passed it on to the disciples. John 10:17-18, John 19:11, and Ephesians 1:18-23 explains that Jesus's authority was given to Him from the Father. In Mark 3:14-15 and Luke 9:1-2, we see Jesus transferring His authority to the disciples, and in Matthew 28:18-20 we read about Jesus transferring the authority His Father gave Him to His followers. I encourage you to study these passages and research more that speak of Jesus's handling of authority.

I have always been intrigued by the fact that even those with authority must remain under authority. If submission does not remain intact, the authority will be misappropriated. Unfortunately, we have seen this happen all too often in the church. Someone is given authority, then after a while he forgets where that authority came from and no longer wants to submit. He believes he is the source!

Understanding true authority is central to empowerment. This aspect of leadership development is meant to flow like a river. Empowerment is supposed to pour out from its source and keep flowing. Empowerment breaks down when it stops at a person.

When it is prevented from flowing freely, it becomes stagnant like a pond. To rightly sustain transferred authority, a leader must be faithful to serve the one who gave him the authority and then pass it on to others.

THE ART OF EMPOWERMENT

Empowering leaders isn't a magic trick. Nor is it a miracle that only a few leaders experience. Empowerment is an art, but it's also measurable. It consists of five clear components that work when a leader is persistent. Empowerment does not allow abandonment. It requires a consistent and committed relationship because it blends guidelines with freedom. Empowerment is like oxygen to a leader. If deprived of it for long, he won't be able to lead. The following five components of empowerment are easy enough to understand, but they won't bear much fruit if they are not consistently put into practice.

1. Trust with responsibility.

When I joined the staff at 12Stone in 2001, I was their first executive pastor. Kevin founded the church, and at that time he had been the senior pastor for fourteen years. Plenty of people wondered whether Kevin would give me the keys. And if he did, would he take them back? I understood that; 12Stone was his baby. He had poured his life into the church. But I'm here to tell you that not only did Kevin give me the keys to executive leadership, but also he has never even temporarily taken them back. He trusted me with tremendous responsibility from day one. I've had complete freedom to lead the staff and

> **Empowerment is like oxygen to leaders.**

ministries of the church. I've tried to give it all back to him a couple times, and he won't take it!

The trust Kevin and I share didn't magically occur. He set guidelines, and we communicated often. In our first week together Kevin said to me, "Do not mess with the culture." That's a big deal. As the senior leader, he has driven certain values into the culture of 12Stone, and it isn't my job to change them. My job is to enhance them. It's my responsibility to incorporate those values into what I do to expand the ministry and develop leaders who embrace the culture of our church.

Part of the trust Kevin had in me came from the twenty years of ministry experience I brought to the table. Trust isn't indiscriminately and automatically given to just anyone. It is a two-way street, and it is earned. A young or inexperienced leader should not expect a blank check and the keys to the kingdom. That said, it is possible to trust someone without giving him responsibility, but it is impossible to empower a person without turning over the reins to some degree. I'll talk more about this later.

When Kevin and I were first establishing trust, we made regular communication a priority. To this day we meet every week for two or three hours, and we participate in a couple of brief retreats each year. We fiercely protect this time because we use it to think, plan, strategize, and stay aligned spiritually and philosophically.

Because the person you trust with leadership responsibility will have a significant influence on the future of your ministry, it is essential that you place the right individual in the right position. We talked about inviting the right person onto your team in chapter 5, but I must underscore this point again because it is so important. Whether the individual is a staff member or a key volunteer, having the right person in the right seat on the bus will make all the difference between success and failure.

When the right person is in place, you must give him permission to lead within his own style and personality as long as he aligns with the vision, values, and culture of the ministry. You must give him permission to make mistakes as long at he learns from them and doesn't repeat those errors. And when he succeeds, celebrate those victories.

This first step of empowerment should not be made with skepticism. Don't stand back with your arms crossed, thinking, "We'll see if he makes it or not." Lean in! Be that leader's biggest supporter! Remember, you selected the individual, so you share in the responsibility of his failure or success. Trusting a leader with real responsibility always requires some risk. And when you actually let the person lead, it can be downright scary! If you've never felt that kind of anxiety, you haven't let go of anything that really matters.

Do you trust other leaders with responsibility? Do you give it to them then take it back? Or do you give them responsibility then leave them to fend for themselves? Leaders who admit to taking back responsibility from those they are mentoring often give the same reason—that the person wasn't competent. But that problem can be easily fixed.

2. Train for competency.

Pastor Miles Welch leads our college and intern ministries at 12Stone. As a former Marine, Miles is perfect for the job. I'm not saying he's a drill sergeant, but he does get the job done. When I was a rookie in ministry, I "practiced" leading in college ministries, and to this day I have great passion for the potential of students. Because of my focus in leadership development, I am very connected to 12Stone's intern ministry. Each time Miles asks me to teach, I'm like a kid in a candy store. I can't wait. I'm thrilled every time I have an opportunity to teach a hundred, or several hundred, pastors. But there's nothing quite like talking with fifteen to twenty interns. They are our future.

At 12Stone we are very committed to equipping and developing all leaders. And that value shows in every ministry the church leads. Being committed to consistent training is essential. I have seen in far too many churches a desire for training but little long-term, consistent follow-through.

Miles and I and several others on the team are involved in training the interns for leadership and ministry competency. Their training involves spiritual intensity objectives and skill set objectives in the following four areas: relational leadership, platform leadership, personal leadership, and organizational leadership. Those areas reflect our biblical and cultural values, and it's important that your training is congruent with your values as well. Our training is a two-year process that is always under innovative development, and God is granting us great results. Young emerging leaders come in with tremendous potential and in two years leave with real ministry experience, training, and vision for new possibilities. Our program focuses primarily on each intern's development, and they practice real ministry in live laboratories.

It would not be enough to trust our young interns with responsibility alone. They must be trained. I'm very much a champion of academic achievement, but without practical training by leaders in the trenches, our young leaders will struggle. Far too many stories are told of college graduates who get eaten alive during their first years in ministry. We intend to train the next generation well, and Miles does a great job leading the way.

The same is true for volunteer leaders. Training for competency is a nonnegotiable. Pastors Mark Eiken and Robin Ritchie do an outstanding job investing in the competency of our small group leaders at 12Stone. Mark trains with the objective of helping the leaders see true transformation in their small group members' lives so they will have God stories, growth stories, and gift stories to share. God stories reveal that God still shows up, miracles still happen, and people's lives are still being changed. Growth stories identify the specific ways the people in each small group are growing—from strengthened marriages to stronger prayer lives. Gift stories tell how the people are using their spiritual gifts to serve in the body of Christ. Each of these stories represents a different focus the leaders must have as they minister to their small groups.

Robin provides a different kind of training that complements Mark's. Robin has a heart for people and prayer and is one the smartest people I know. She also has a remarkable gift for "training in the trenches." She will visit a small group in action and teach the leader to identify new apprentice leaders. After small group meetings, Robin will talk with the leaders to assess the health and strength of the group, then coach them through any challenges. By being there in the small group meeting, Robin brings "leadership eyes" to the room and shows the small group leader how to do the same.

I can't leave the issue of training without mentioning the financial investment required. Like most things in the local church, it is possible to get creative and stretch your training dollars if you have a limited budget. Don't get hung up on the amount spent. What's important is that you create a budget to equip and develop leaders.

Competency is not static. Each leader begins with the basics but continues to improve throughout the course of his life. So please do not see this step or any of the five steps of empowerment as something you can mark off your check list. Empowerment is an ongoing process.

3. Unleash with authority.

I've already mentioned that all authority is transferred, but it can't be transferred if you won't release it. This third part of the empowerment process asks you to do a gut check, and here it is: Are you willing to share your authority? If you are honest, you'll admit it's difficult to share leadership authority. Comparatively, it's easy to give away responsibility. After all, this reduces your workload. But giving away authority cuts into how much control you have.

I'm not talking about the negative kind of control that authoritarian leaders are known for. I'm talking about the kind of control leaders exercise to manage an organization. Leaders guide and direct ministries for the good of the people they serve. This is part of their job. Because leaders care about the people they serve and the results of ministry, and because they have been carrying the responsibility of leadership for some time, releasing authority can be difficult.

When it comes to releasing leaders, the level of authority they're given must equal their responsibility. Tim Jones and Luis Ramos were the head ushers for 12Stone's two services when we moved into our current facility at the Central campus. John Burgess joined the team of head ushers, or "service leaders," when we later launched a third service. John, Tim, and Luis do a great job, but they have very different personalities. They have different leadership styles, but each man is effective.

One thing they have in common is the authority they have

been given to get the job done. They recruit ushers, place them on teams, improvise when changes are made in the service, organize a smooth and effective offering, manage difficult moments including medical emergencies, and much more. So much happens on a Sunday morning, even between services, and the head ushers must have the authority to deal with any of it.

Let me be clear about something. Releasing authority doesn't mean there is no need for teamwork or communication. Tim, John, and Luis work closely with Pastor Mark Eiken, but Mark gives them authority to lead. In order for this to become a reality in your ministry, your organization must develop a leadership culture that embraces boldness over caution. When the leaders on your team know you support them, they will lead with much more boldness. If you are a heavy-handed leader, second-guess your team members, or micromanage them, the leaders will revert into a very cautious mode. Some may quit leading all together.

There will be times when you should reclaim the authority you released, but those times should be rare. Those times will fall into two main categories. The first is when an executive decision needs to be made. Sometimes, for example, the church board or the senior pastor must make a decision that affects the individuals overseeing the staff and volunteer leaders. This is normal but usually not frequent. In this situation, the leader is not actually removing authority from a leader. The board or senior leaders are simply exercising their authority.

The second category is when the new leader demonstrates a consistently bad attitude or pattern of poor performance. What is key here is that there is a sustained pattern of unacceptable behavior. All leaders make mistakes, have bad days, and experience difficult seasons. That is not a call for their authority to be removed.

They need to be coached through the rough patches. Only when the leader consistently demonstrates a poor attitude or performance—and lacks a willingness to learn or change—should you rescind his authority. And when ministry results begin to decline to the extent that the organization's mission and goals are being compromised, you are compelled to pull his authority. Ideally, the leader's authority will be restored, but the process takes time.

4. Communicate clear expectations.

So far we have trusted the emerging leader with responsibility, trained him to build competency, and unleashed him with authority. The next step is to make your expectations clear. You're sure to demotivate a leader—and I mean truly let the wind out of his sails—if you fail to agree upon your expectations. As a leader, you may like to keep things open-ended—to call an audible when you need to—but you will drive your leaders crazy if they don't know what you want. This all starts with *you* knowing what you want! Far too often the "supervising" leader isn't confident about which direction to take or where to set priorities. If this is the case with you, something must change. You can't expect the leaders you are developing to guess what you want.

Assuming you do know what you want from those you lead, I strongly recommend you put those expectations in writing. They can be changed as long as you don't revise them too often. But it is important that the expectations be written down. I've attended many meetings where two people had a great conversation and thought they agreed upon the same thing, but later learned they were not on the same page.

Write your expectations down. You don't have to make this complicated. A simple bullet-point list of measurable goals should easily fit on one page, and your volunteer leaders will thank you for it. Trust me. Unlike staff, volunteer leaders have their own careers to tend to and don't have unlimited time to meet all the goals on your list.

I want to underscore the importance of creating a list with succinct bullet points. Long, wordy paragraphs typically cloud the issue and are hardly read. Using bullet points helps you think much more clearly, and they actually draw readers in.

Writing down expectations is the foundation for clear communication. Yet while your communication will be based on what was written, most of it should be live and ongoing. You and your emerging leaders should talk often. Keep the lines of communication open. And above all, be honest. Speak the truth and don't sugarcoat issues. When expectations are not being met, say something. Assume the best from your apprentice leaders, but say something if a problem arises.

A good first approach is to ask a question, even if the answer seems obvious. First ask the emerging leader if he or she sees the problem and agrees with you about its impact. You'd be surprised how diverse perspectives can be. If you don't see the situation the same way and agree that improvement is needed, then all the coaching and mentoring in the world won't help.

I would be remiss if I didn't mention a strange component I've noticed in the local church. It is the elevation of faithfulness over results. We have a tendency to be soft on leaders, especially volunteer leaders. But this doesn't help them or the ministry. I'm not suggesting you become mean. The people who serve in ministry make it possible for us to fulfill the mission. However, there is a difference between extending grace and lowering your standards. Never lower your standards. Keep the bar high and challenge apprentice leaders to stretch to reach it. If you have done a good job communicating your expectations, there will be no reason to lower them.

Leadership is an artful combination of vision, direction, and strategy, and it is loaded with expectations. Whether those expectations are met can make or break a leader. The more clearly you communicate, the better and more effective your leadership will be.

5. Let apprentices know you love and believe in them.

If you know how it feels for someone to believe in you, then you are aware that no price tag can be put on that kind of support. The person who gave you your first job or leadership position believed in you. And if you were truly blessed, that individual loved and cared for you as well. This is a priceless gift. And if that person sticks with you when you are struggling, supports you, and helps you get through the difficult times, it's almost impossible to describe what that really means. When I think of the people who have believed in me through the years, I experience a profound sense of gratitude that words can't describe.

This is the potential impact the last component of the empowerment process carries. It is possible to empower apprentice leaders using only the first four elements we have discussed so far, but that is like launching a space shuttle with the fuel tanks half-full. The shuttle just won't go as far. The entire process of empowerment is more art than science, but this last component comes from the heart and will go directly to your apprentice's.

It is not softhearted or weak to care about someone. It's no more soft than a parent who loves his or her child. If you've had teenagers, you understand tough love! If your children are still young, hang on. You'll have your turn! Parents look out for the best interest of their children. Leaders who empower emerging leaders do the same. The mission is critical, but if you don't genuinely care about the leaders you empower, you compromise the core of the mission. Jesus died for the people. He modeled love as the cornerstone of our faith. I fully acknowledge the realities of the natural realm, but that should never eclipse genuinely caring about the leaders you develop and empower.

This kind of godly love requires us to be honest even when it hurts. A friend of mine was mentoring a new leader who serves as the senior pastor of a church of about five hundred people. I'll call my friend Jim and the pastor Ken. The church is cutting-edge and gutsy like its pastor. Ken is bold and full of passion. He's a type A, driven leader, and takes no prisoners.

During a stewardship campaign, Ken's personality landed him in hot water. A couple of key leaders accused him not of misappropriating funds, but of spinning his communication about the money to make the church's financial position look different from the reality. It was all completely innocent, but perception is everything. The church followed Ken, but his hard-charging, no-nonsense style caused just enough "normal" friction within the congregation for these two key leaders to turn things against Ken.

The situation became ugly. The leaders began to hold secret meetings and literally tore the church apart. Jim believed in Ken, yet he went to him and said that though he is a good and godly man, the church no longer trusted him. It hurt Ken deeply to hear those words. He considered leaving the ministry. Ken owned his mistakes, but he didn't understand why his people would turn on him.

Jim continued to believe in Ken and stuck with him. Jim even spoke the painful truth about how he needed to improve as a leader. It's a long and complicated story, and the situation took a couple of years to play out, but the church is back on track and stronger than ever with Ken still serving in leadership.

When you believe in someone, you make a statement of faith that travels from your heart to theirs. You believe in who they are, and you believe in what they can do. It is not uncommon in the early stages of development and empowering (and especially during the selection and inclusion phase) for you to believe in someone more than he believes in himself. When you believe in someone, you deposit personal faith and confidence into his leadership. I am forever grateful to those who believed in me. I am a changed person because of them. My prayer is that those you believe in will be changed for the good and live an extraordinary life.

AMPLIFY YOUR LEADERSHIP

Establish a Relationship	→	Engage a Follower	→	Embrace a Team Member	→	Coach an Apprentice	→	Mentor a New Leader
• *Connect* at the heart • *Appreciate* people for who they are		• *Encourage* people to bring out their best • *Inspire* people to follow the vision		• *Invite* individuals into meaningful ministry • *Equip* team members for ministry success		• *Select* the best potential leaders • *Include* emerging leaders to give them relevant experience		• *Develop* new leaders because the process changes lives • *Empower* effective leaders to realize their potential

The *Amplified Leadership* process is one you can devote your life to. It's not flashy, but it works. Developing leaders takes time, but it's worth it. You'll receive deep personal satisfaction when you see the leaders you've developed standing next to other leaders, and the results for God's kingdom will be amazing. Remember, the idea is to take this leadership process and continue to develop new leaders. Don't stop after you have empowered your first leader. You're not done. The process is designed to keep going! From continually establishing relationships to empowering leaders, you should keep increasing and expanding your leadership by developing other leaders so that your church is stronger and the kingdom is larger.

When you develop people to lead those who serve in ministry, you are *adding* leaders. It's not just you leading. That's very good, but here's where it can become truly captivating. When you continue the process, and other leaders you have developed also pour into new leaders, now you are *multiplying* leaders. The results become exponential! There's no stopping the potential of your church as that takes place over time.

My hope and prayer is that you benefit from what I've learned, and that you take this process and practice it for many years to come. When the practices and skills become second nature to you, add your own ideas to the mix. Write me with your suggestions to enhance the process. I promise, I will read your e-mails and letters! I have one word of caution: Don't try to shorten the process. That's the great temptation, to try to speed things up. Leadership development doesn't work that way. It takes time.

If you learn these practices, consistently live them out, and, I hope, add your own insights to them, I'm convinced your leadership will be amplified and the Great Commission will be advanced. I offer this simple prayer of blessing for you and all the new leaders who will enter the ring because you took the time to invest in them.

Lord Jesus, bless the leaders who are reading this book. Grant them unusual favor as they lead the ministries they serve. Bless them with the courage to lead, the wisdom to know what to do, and the joy needed to stay in the ring and keep fighting. Bring potential leaders to the right church and cause them to rise up to serve You well. I pray the process in this book would serve as a helpful guide that results in many new leaders. And, Father, may the ultimate result of their leadership be that many people give their hearts to You for their salvation. In the name of Jesus, amen.

NOTES

INTRODUCTION

1. *Cinderella Man*, directed by Ron Howard (Universal City, CA: Universal Studios, 2005), DVD.

PART ONE

1. John Maxwell, *The Treasure of a Friend* (Nashville, TN: Thomas Nelson, 1999), 73.

2. Ibid, 60.

PART TWO

1. James MacGregor Burns, *Leadership* (New York: Harper & Row, 1978), 427.

CHAPTER THREE

1. Rick Warren, senior pastor, Saddleback Church, in discussion with the author, September 2011.

CHAPTER FOUR

1. Crossroads of Arlington Church, About Us, "Joe Centineo, Senior Pastor," http://www.crossroadsofarlington.org/about-us/our-staff/joe-centineo/ (accessed June 22, 2011).

2. This quote is often attributed to Charles Spurgeon, but it is derived from several sermons he preached. The quote, "God is too wise to err, too good to be unkind; leave off doubting him, and begin to trust him, for in so doing, thou wilt put a crown on his head, but in doubting him thou dost trample his crown beneath thy feet, " was said during a 1857 sermon titled "Fear Not" (Royal Surrey Gardens, London, England, October 4, 1857), http://www .spurgeon.org/sermons/0156.htm (accessed July 7, 2011).

CHAPTER SIX

1. William Barclay, *The Daily Bible Study Series: Letters to the Galatians and Ephesians*, revised edition (Philadelphia, PA: The Westminster Press, 1976), 149; E. K. Simpson and F. F. Bruce, *The New International Commentary on the New Testament: The Epistle to the Ephesians and Colossians*, 10th printing (Grand Rapids, MI: Wm. B. Eerdmans Publishing, 1979), 93; *Matthew Henry's Commentary* (Grand Rapids, MI: Zondervan, 1961), 1853.

PART FOUR

1. Bill Carter, "'The Apprentice' Scores Ratings Near Top for the Season," *New York Times*, April 17, 2004, http://www.nytimes.com/2004/04/17/us/the -apprentice-scores-ratings-near-top-for-the-season.html (accessed July 7, 2011).

Dan would love to hear from you. You can write to him at
dan.reiland@12Stone.com.
To read his blog, which is packed with practical
and helpful leadership material, visit **http://danreiland.com.**

Other resources by Dan Reiland:

Shoulder to Shoulder: Strengthening Your Church by Supporting Your Pastor. This book will help leaders and potential team members understand the uniqueness of ministry, as well as become more effective in serving while supporting the pastor's vision. This book is ideal for churches with eight hundred or less in attendance. It is highly recommended for board members, new members, small group leaders, and other volunteer leaders.

Joshua's Men Training Curriculum: A One-Year Process to Raise Up Spiritual Leaders. This CD resource will give men an intensive leadership development experience. It is best used in one or two small groups a year that meet monthly and are led by a seasoned leader and/or the pastor of the church. The curriculum is available at www.INJOY.com.

Dan Reiland is the executive pastor of 12Stone Church in Lawrenceville, Georgia. He previously spent twenty years serving in ministry with Dr. John C. Maxwell, first as executive pastor of Skyline Wesleyan Church in San Diego, California, then as vice president of Leadership and Church Development at INJOY based out of Atlanta. Dan is known as a leader with a pastor's heart. He truly loves the local church but is also described as one of the nation's most innovative church thinkers and pastors' coaches. Dan and his family live in suburban Atlanta.